What Is
New Testament
Theology?

Guides to Biblical Scholarship
New Testament Series

What Is
New Testament
Theology?

Dan O. Via

Fortress Press
Minneapolis

Book design by Beth Wright

The publisher gratefully acknowledges the following for permission to reprint material previously published by the author: Trinity Press International for material from *The Revelation of God and/as Human Reception*; *Perspectives in Religious Studies* for material from "New Testament Theology: Historical Event, Literary Text, and the Locus of Revelation" (19:4 [1992] 369–88); and Edwin Mellen Press for material from "New Testament Theology: Historical Event, Literary Text, and the Locus of Revelation," in *Perspectives on Contemporary New Testament Questions*, ed. Edgar V. McKnight (1992).

Library of Congress Cataloging-in-Publication Data

Via, Dan Otto, date–
    What is New Testament theology? / Dan O. Via.
        p.   cm. — (Guides to biblical scholarship)
    Includes bibliographical references and indexes.
    ISBN 0-8006-3263-X (pbk. : alk. paper)
        1. Bible. N.T.—Theology. 2. Bible. N.T.—Criticism, interpretation, etc.
    I. Title. II. Series.

BS2397 .V53 2002
230'.0415—dc21
                                                    2002070112

Manufactured in the U.S.A.   AF 1-3263

Contents

The Legacy of Hendrikus Boers

In 1979 Hendrikus Boers published an excellent book in this series under the same title as that of the present work. His treatment of the issues, however, has been out of print for several years; therefore, it seems worthwhile to ask the question again, in the context of the same series: What is New Testament theology?

Boers's Contribution

It is appropriate here at the outset to indicate in a very summary way something of Boers's contribution and my relationship to it.

Boers refers to the practice of theology in a way that suggests two possible levels of formality. Building on Alfred North Whitehead's definition of philosophy, Boers defined theology as "a coherent, logical, necessary system of general ideas in terms of which every element of our experience concerning matters relating to God can be interpreted" (1979:13). In Scholasticism, Christianity developed an understanding of theology that was close to the definition just mentioned (14–16).

Boers uses the adjective *theological* to refer in a more general sense to every statement about God or every religious expression insofar as it may constitute material for theology in the first sense (13).

I am inclined to think that most of the theology in the New Testament itself belongs to the second level, while most scholarly treatments of New Testament theology belong in a broad and inexact sense to the first. My concern in this book is to consider the diverse ways in which various New Testament scholars in recent decades have sought to bring the incipient theological potential in the New Testament to disciplined, structured expression.

Boers gives a helpful analysis of Johann Philip Gabler (1753–1826), who is generally credited with having established biblical theology as a separate discipline, independent of dogmatic theology. Boers discusses three illuminating distinctions that Gabler made and uses one of them to structure his own analysis of twentieth-century New Testament theology (Boers 1979:24–35).

Religion is *divine* teaching in ordinary, simple language while *theology* is a *human* achievement, a systematic and sophisticated development. Religion is concerned with the unchanging, but theology is contingent and changing (Gabler 1980:135–36).

The purpose of *biblical theology* is to mediate between biblical religion and dogmatic theology. Its subject matter is the former, but its method is theological, a systematizing of the teachings of biblical religion. The conclusions of biblical theology should be free of dogmatic determinants. It is a historical discipline that seeks to clarify what the biblical texts taught in their historical context. *Dogmatic theology*, on the other hand, has a present, didactic purpose, philosophizing about all matters related to God—on the basis of pure biblical theology, but contingent upon the ability and cultural setting of the theologian. Thus dogmatic theology is always changing. Biblical theology is not an end in itself but is intended to provide a basis for dogmatic theology (Gabler 1980:137–39, 142).

True biblical theology is a systematic description of all the elements of biblical religion. *Pure biblical theology* identifies and eliminates contingent elements in biblical religion, leaving only a system of unchanging concepts as a basis for dogmatic theology.

Boers then categorizes William Wrede, Wilhelm Bousset, Johann Weiss, and Adolf Schlatter—despite real differences among them—under the rubric of true New Testament theology. I will discuss Wrede in chapters 3 and 4 below. Boers takes Rudolf Bultmann and Herbert Braun as exemplars of pure New Testament theology.

Bultmann developed a pure theology of the New Testament—at least of Paul and John—in that he purged the ever-timely content of its contingent, time-conditioned form of expression—myth (Boers 1979:75–80). Bultmann will be discussed in later chapters.

Herbert Braun followed Bultmann but modified the latter's project in two ways. He took a step beyond Bultmann in the direction of developing a scheme to systemize New Testament theology as a whole. And, in order to break the hold that an interpreter's presuppositions have in interpretation, Braun placed the articulation of New Testament theology more integrally within the analysis of Hellenistic religions (Boers 1979:80–84).

For Braun the problem of New Testament theology is twofold. If we take theology broadly as dealing with several themes, then the New Testament writers disagree with one another on any given theme. The themes that Braun would use to systematize New Testament theology are Christology, salvation, the place of the law, eschatology, and the sacraments. If, on the other hand, one understands theology more narrowly as the teaching about God or the divine world, then the problem is that the New Testament represents God in a way that is alien to us. God appears mythologically as an objectively fixed given "out there" independent of us, existing in and for God's own self.

Braun hopes to resolve both of these problems with one hermeneutical move. God is to be understood not as the separate other but as the power that impinges upon us out of our common humanity, creating the present moment as a crisis, keeping our existence in meaningful motion by both making a radical demand upon us and accepting us unconditionally as we are. This reconceptualizing of God in existential terms also suggests a way to resolve the problem of theological differences among the several New Testament figures. These conflicting positions are at the level of *theological concepts.* But at a deeper level the reconceptualizing of God is an *understanding of human existence* that establishes an incipient element of agreement among the several writers (Braun 1965; 1968). There is a good question about whether Braun's particular mode of demythologizing actually preserves the true transcendence of God (see Braun 1979:122–36).

Transition to the Present Work

I will not deal with all of the figures that Boers discusses, nor will I use his organizing principle. His fine contribution, while out of print, is available in libraries.

Perhaps the primary connecting link between Boers's discussion and mine is the importance of Rudolf Bultmann. It is, of course, the case that many New Testament scholars and theologians consider Bultmann to belong to our recent past and not to the contemporary theological and hermeneutical dialogue. There are, to be sure, significant ways in which Bultmann's program needs to be criticized, reworked, and amplified. This will be brought out in later chapters. But there are also themes in Bultmann's works that we forget at our peril. And one can cite important voices that, although they are critical of Bultmann, take his contribution to be of such a magnitude that we can still build on it and/or should be in dialogue with it (Soelle 1974; Jones 1991; Adam 1995a; Donahue 1996). Reginald H. Fuller judges that while the historical reconstructions in Bultmann's *Theology of the New Testament* are now dated, the theological questions that it raises are still very much alive (Fuller 1989:567).

The next chapter will display several different ways of organizing a theology of the New Testament. The primary issue to be pursued in this book, however, is not how to structure a New Testament theology but how to identify and articulate theological meanings found in the New Testament, whether one is dealing with a small text, a large text, or the whole of the New Testament canon. How does one discipline the movement from the theological potential found in the New Testament to theological articulation structured in some way? Structure has a bearing on meaning; but for the sake of analysis, I will distinguish the overview of organizational possibilities from the question of the hermeneutics of theological meaning.

My scheme for giving order to the hermeneutical quest will be two questions about how one does New Testament theology, along with several answers that have been given to these questions over the last few decades. (1) Does New Testament theology deal with the text of the New Testament or with something outside of the text—such as the unfolding of early Christian religion, the events of salvation history, the historical Jesus in particular, or an understanding of human existence? (2) Is New Testament theology a strictly historical project, a dialectical interaction between historical interpretation and hermeneutical concerns, or a solely hermeneutical program? My approach to the answers given to these questions by several scholars will be in considerable part descriptive, but there will also be critical and advocative elements.

In this immediate context, by a "historical project" I mean the intention to give an objective, descriptive account of the early Christian life-in-faith process or of the meaning of the New Testament texts in their first-century context. By a "hermeneutical program" I mean interpretation that acknowledges the proper role of the interpreter's presuppositions, pre-understanding, or social location and that seeks to show that the text can address our present situation as a living summons. When I speak in this context of New Testament theology as being both historical *and* hermeneutical, or historical *or* hermeneutical, I am implying a principled distinction between historical and hermeneutical and suggesting that historical interpretation is *not* hermeneutical. When I do that, I am assuming the position of those historical interpreters who believe that historical inquiry is highly objective and can escape the subjectivity of the interpreter. But as my discussion develops, and especially in the last chapters, I will argue that historical interpretation is hermeneutical, that is, that historians in their reconstructions of the past do give expression to their own pre-understanding, imagination, interests, and the force of their social location.

2

The Structuring of
New Testament Theology

Let us look selectively at several ways in which New Testament theology or Christology has been organized in the latter half of the twentieth century. These works are in name and/or actuality treatments of the New Testament as a whole. While discussion of hermeneutical issues will not be addressed focally until later chapters, it would be artificial not to give some attention in this chapter to occasional hermeneutical issues that arise here. It may be true that there are two basic ways of organizing a New Testament theology—the thematic and the historical-chronological (Fuller 1989:577)—but these two methods, as well as their interweaving, may be elaborated in various ways.

Rudolf Bultmann

In *Theology of the New Testament* (2 vols., 1951; 1955a), Rudolf Bultmann's overall plan is a historical unfolding, and the progression is largely, though not entirely, chronological. The categories that are foregrounded and that define the primary units of the structure are individuals and limited period-situations. The outline that results is as follows: (1) the Message of Jesus, (2) the Kerygma of the Earliest Church, (3) the Kerygma of the Hellenistic Church aside from Paul, (4) the Theology of Paul, (5) the Theology of the Gospel of John and Johannine Epistles, (6) the Development toward the Ancient Church. Bultmann attends to the historical situations from which the kerygmatic and theological themes of these several sections emerge and points to interconnections and developments among these parts.

A consideration of two Bultmannian themes will enable us to understand why all of the parts of the structure do not get the same kind of treatment although they all belong to the historical stream. The first is Bultmann's judgment that John and Paul most adequately present the New Testament's kerygmatic norm: that the saving occurrence in Jesus is simultaneously eschatological and historical (1955a:123–27). Paul and John are his canon within the canon. The second is Bultmann's distinction between two ways of grasping history. History as *Historie* is the past as reconstructed by scholars and as remaining in the past. History as *Geschichte* is the past as still impinging upon the present (1964:30; 1969:241). As it turns out for Bultmann, the theologies of Paul and John belong to *Geschichte,* while the other units in his structure belong to *Historie.* The theologies of Paul and John are articulated as a viable option for twentieth-century people while the ideas in the other segments remain interesting ideas of the past.

Although the first chapter in Bultmann's *Theology of the New Testament* is "The Message of Jesus," Bultmann begins by declaring that the message is not part of the theology itself but is rather a presupposition for it (1951:3). Bultmann says this in considerable part because for him the theology in the New Testament is the drawing out of the element of understanding in the response of faith to the early Christian proclamation of Jesus' death and resurrection (1955a:237–41). There can be no theology in the proper sense prior to the proclamation of Jesus' death and resurrection and the faith awakened by this proclamation. The historical Jesus remains in the historical past and does not evoke faith in the present (1964:30).

One could argue, however, that the teaching and action of the historical Jesus are as evocative of faith as is the kerygma of his death and resurrection and that this faith is existentially viable for our time. In fact, Bultmann, despite himself, seems to make such a claim for the word of the historical Jesus in *Jesus and the Word* (1958a:212–19).

My book, *The Revelation of God and/as Human Reception,* is by no means a full theology of the New Testament, but it is a more or less comprehensive treatment of one important theme. The structure of the central chapters resembles Bultmann's—the historical

Jesus, Paul, Mark, Matthew, and John. It is distinguished from Bultmann's approach by the fact that Mark and Matthew are given focal attention and are treated as having the same authority and hermeneutical power in principle as Paul and John. The significance of the Synoptic narratives will be discussed further in the next chapter.

In the book just mentioned I have enclosed the New Testament material between an Introduction and a Conclusion and Appendix that deal with revelation in recent systematic theology. Thus, New Testament theology and systematic theology are made to be in dialogue with each other, and the former is treated as a primary source and norm for the latter. In this regard I belong to the tradition of J. P. Gabler and Adolph Schlatter (see Fuller 1989:574–75) and display a trait that Reginald H. Fuller surmised would characterize New Testament theology around the turn of the millennium (Fuller 1989:578).

Joachim Jeremias

In comparison with Bultmann, the situation is quite different with Joachim Jeremias, *New Testament Theology* (1971). It is clear that for him the historical Jesus is very much an ingredient in New Testament theology itself. The subtitle of the volume is "The Proclamation of Jesus," which the title page of the original German indicates is to be a "First Part." No other parts appeared, however. Therefore, our discussion of the structure of Jeremias' New Testament theology is dependent on this volume.

Jeremias's *New Testament Theology* has a seven-part structure: (1) How Reliable Is the Tradition of the Sayings of Jesus? (2) The Mission of Jesus, (3) The Dawn of the Time of Salvation, (4) The Period of Grace, (5) The New People of God, (6) Jesus' Testimony to His Mission, and (7) Easter.

The first two items in the outline are historical in nature: In the first we have Jeremias's argument that the Jesus tradition is substantially reliable: the burden of proof is on those who would show historical inauthenticity, not on those who would claim authenticity (1971:1, 37). This reverses the position of the Bultmann school. In the second section Jeremias seeks to find a grounding for Jesus' proclamation in an event, in an experience of Jesus' life that preceded the preaching.

That event centers on the baptism of Jesus. Jesus had followed John and had a very high estimate of him. But in his baptism by John, Jesus experienced a call to a mission and message significantly different from John's. Here Jesus became conscious of being in the grasp of the Spirit and of being God's servant in the sense of Isaiah 42:1. Also at this point, Jesus became aware of being in a singular father-son relationship with God (Matt 11:27; Luke 10:22). This discussion focuses on Jesus' use of the Aramaic word *'Abba* as his word for Father, an intimate term used by children for their earthly fathers. Jeremias believes that in this call Jesus was given a full revelation that he alone was in a position to pass on to others. Jeremias further argues that behind the temptation stories is a historical nucleus that represents Jesus' acceptance of his mission. In accepting his call, he renounced political messiahship and rejected the avoidance of suffering. From this multifaceted experience flowed Jesus' proclamation.

The proclamation, as we saw above, is structured by means of five theological themes. Toward the end, Jeremias turns again to more specifically historical questions. Did the historical Jesus make interpretative statements about his death? Yes, there is a historical nucleus. What was the nature of the Easter "events" (1971:276–99)? The earliest accounts did not understand the resurrection appearances in a materialistic way (300–11).

Although Jeremias did not complete his *New Testament Theology*, we can conjecture how it *might* have unfolded from his earlier short book, *The Central Message of the New Testament* (1965). Here the structuring units are theological themes. The first chapter, Abba, is taken up into the *New Testament Theology*. The second chapter, The Sacrificial Death, traces the significance of Jesus' death back from Hebrews, 1 Peter, and Paul to Jesus. Chapter 3, Justification by Faith, deals mainly with Paul; and chapter 4, The Revealing Word, deals primarily with the prologue of John.

James D. G. Dunn

We have a still different kind of structure in James D. G. Dunn's *Unity and Diversity in the New Testament* (1977). A second edition with a long, new foreword (1989) is able to take account of scholarly developments since 1977 but does not change the structure.

Dunn begins with an introductory chapter (I) that raises a theological question: What is the status of the concept of orthodoxy? He then transforms this into the less problematic question: Was there a uniform strand in earliest Christianity that identifies what is authentically Christian? Next, there follow thirteen chapters that present a rigorously historical account of the substance of the theology of the New Testament. Dunn employs two themes or interpretative categories to organize his grasp of the historical reality of early Christianity: Part One—Unity in Diversity; Part Two—Diversity in Unity. Part One seeks unity within the diversity, while Part Two seeks to map out the scope of the diversity (1977:7).

The first chapters of Part One display diversities within different kinds of material or theological expression: II. Kerygmata or Proclamations; III. Confessional Formulae; IV. Tradition; and V. Old Testament Exegesis. The remaining chapters of Part One discuss diversities within several theological themes: VI. Ministry; VII. Worship; VIII. Sacraments; IX. Spirit and Experience; and X. Christology. Among diversities Dunn notes, for example, that Jesus' proclamation called on people to decide for the kingdom of God while the various early church proclamations summoned people to faith in Jesus (1977:14–15, 22). Similarly, the earliest Christology focused on Jesus' resurrection and future appearance while later Christologies pushed the decisive christological moment back to Jesus' baptism, virginal conception, and preexistence (217–20). At one point Dunn acknowledges that some of the diversities constitute incompatibilities (26), but in the 1989 Foreword he does not allow that these incompatibilities amount to contradictions (xxi).

Repeatedly Dunn asserts that the one element of unity amidst the many diversities is the consistent affirmation of continuity between Jesus of Nazareth and the exalted Christ (59, 172, 201, 203, 216, 227–28, 337, 369, 374, 376).

As his vantage point for developing Part Two, he looks back from the four basic types of Christianity extant in the latter half of the second century and asks what their first-century antecedents were (xxvii). This generates his discussion of the New Testament evidence for four different ways of understanding faith, theology, and practice: XI. Jewish Christianity; XII. Hellenistic Christianity; XIII. Apocalyptic Christianity; and XIV. Early Catholicism. These four types are not mutually exclusive but rather display significant overlapping. Dunn also deals with the New Testament's developing criteria for identifying unacceptable ranges of diversity (265–66, 281–83, 288, 292–95, 304–8, 358–59, 360).

As Dunn began with a theological question, so he ends with one: XV. The Authority of the Canon. He affirms that authority, but, given the magnitude of the diversity, acknowledges the inevitability of any Christian group's operating with a canon within the canon. The one canonical element that could be the norm for all Christian groups is the New Testament's principle of unity: the continuity of Jesus and the exalted Christ (374–78, 383–84). This is not so much a canon within the canon as the canon through the canon (382).

There is a revealing contrast between Bultmann's twofold structuring of Paul's theology—Man Prior to the Revelation of Faith and Man under Faith—and Dunn's twofold structuring of New Testament theology as a whole—Unity in Diversity and Diversity in Unity. Bultmann's structure foregrounds the significance of Paul's texts for a contemporary understanding of human existence, while Dunn's foregrounds the conceptual and practical relationships among the texts themselves and what they refer to in their first-century settings.

Unity and Diversity

The relationship of unity to diversity in the New Testament, to which Dunn made an important contribution, has recently been a prominent question in New Testament theology more broadly. Gerhard F. Hasel, in his *New Testament Theology: Basic Issues,* surveyed the scene up to the late 1970s and discussed various categories that have been offered for grasping the center and unity of the New Testament; for example: anthropology, salvation history, and Christology (1978:140, 144, 148, 155). It is Hasel's opinion that no one structuring principle is deep and wide enough to grasp the theology of the New Testament. Nevertheless, it is the ultimate objective of New Testament theology to draw out of concealment the unity that can bind together divergent testimonies of the New Testament books (163–64, 218).

In 1975 Norman Perrin gave a lecture in which he set out the structure and major concerns of a full-scale New Testament theology that he hoped to write (1984:424) but was prevented by his premature death from carrying out. That lecture was published posthumously in *The Journal of Religion* in 1984.

Perrin intended to write a New Testament theology and not just a history of early Christian religion. Moreover, he proposes to articulate a New Testament *theology* (singular) and not just to review the several *theologies* in the New Testament (413–15). In order to write a theology of the New Testament, it is necessary to identify the unifying principle within the diversity of the New Testament texts (415). Perrin's central thesis is that the unity is provided by the faith image or perspectival image of Jesus. The central concern of the New Testament is not the historical Jesus of the past but *Jesus Christ.* The unifying factor is the synthesis of the remembered Jesus of the past and the faith perspective on that Jesus that emerges from the communities' present experience of the Spirit and the risen Christ (418, 423, 429, 431).

Perrin agrees with Bultmann that the historical Jesus is the presupposition of New Testament theology and not an integral part of it (417). Therefore, he is critical of the central role that Jeremias gives to the Jesus of history (415–17). But Perrin also criticizes Bultmann for achieving not a theology of the New Testament, but a theology of Paul and John (417). He contends that especially early apocalyptic Christianity and the theologies of

Mark, Matthew, and Luke should be treated in principle with the same theological seriousness that is accorded to Paul and John. A proper New Testament theology then would show how the various theological systems in the New Testament configure the interpreted faith image of Jesus (420–31).

Peter Balla in his 1997 book, *Challenges to New Testament Theology,* reviews the discussion of the unity question and develops a position of his own. He acknowledges the strong attacks of many scholars on the theological unity of the New Testament (148, 155–56, 177–79, 208), but he himself persistently maintains that the theology of the New Testament is a unified whole. While there are differences among the writers, these do not amount to contradictions, nor is there any substantial development (161–62, 164–66, 168, 170, 179, 181–83, 185, 196, 199, 205–6, 222–23). Balla argues tentatively that the unifying structure that provides the New Testament with a "basic theology" was of a creedal type. All of the writers whose works are contained in the New Testament adhered to the creed and believed that they were within its boundaries. This unanimously held basic theology is most likely what later turned out to be orthodoxy (77, 85, 201–9, 252–53).

I would like to think that hypothetically speaking if there were a unifying configuration in the New Testament, there could be elements lying outside of this configuration with regard to which different New Testament writers would have had contradictory positions. And a New Testament theology would take account of that phenomenon (Via 1990:133–37). Balla, however, does not concede the presence of contradictions nor the legitimacy of a "canon within the canon" (222)—and for at least two reasons.

If there were contradictory theologies in the New Testament, according to Balla, it would not be possible to write a *theology* (singular) of the New Testament. One could only talk about New Testament *theologies* (plural), and so the enterprise of New Testament theology would be threatened (3, 148–49, 155–56, 177, 179, 208). Since Balla is committed to justifying the enterprise of New Testament *theology* (3, 253–54), he is methodologically, if not dogmatically, constrained to find an essentially unbroken unity in the New Testament.

Balla also evidently believes that contradictions in the New Testament could not have been accommodated within the same canon, confession of faith, and fellowship (186). But I would think it not self-evident that the Christian community—then or now—could not tolerate contradictory positions on some issues if there was unity on certain crucial affirmations.

N. T. Wright

In 1992 N. T. Wright published the first volume of a proposed five-volume work that he would acknowledge, at least tentatively, as a New Testament theology: (1) Introduction, (2) Jesus, (3) Paul, (4) the Gospels, and (5) Conclusion. Thus far the first two have appeared: *The New Testament and the People of God* (1992) and *Jesus and the Victory of God* (1996). The structuring units of the three central parts of the project are historically identifiable individual figures or groups of texts. This organization is reminiscent of Bultmann's. Wright's intention is to offer a synthesis of the major parts of the New Testament in light of an expansive hypothesis, a synthesis that will avoid, on the one hand, the unserviceable brevity of one-volume theologies of the New Testament and, on the other hand, the unduly extended treatments of limited subareas (1992:xiii–xiv, 18–28).

While Bultmann wrote expansively about hermeneutical issues, his *Theology of the New Testament* itself contains relatively little explicit discussion of his hermeneutical approach. Wright, on the other hand, lays out his hermeneutical position at length in the first volume. Part I gives an overview of his approach. His aim is to integrate a traditional Christian concern about theological meaning with modern historical analysis and an attentiveness to the readers' contribution to textual meaning, which Wright calls postmodern. This program governs the structure of the remainder of the book.

Part II addresses in a theoretical and philosophical way the issues of how knowledge is acquired and the nature of literature, history, and theology. Part III deals concretely with the context of first century Christianity in the Judaism of the Greco-Roman world. Then in Part IV, Wright discusses in summary fashion the theology of the main New Testament witnesses. Throughout all the parts he puts a great deal of stress on the role of story in bringing the New Testament vision to expression. The conclusion in Part V raises the essential theological issue: the question of God.

In the Introduction (Part I) of *Jesus and the Victory of God*, Wright discusses several aspects of the contemporary quest for the historical Jesus. Then in two central parts he grasps Jesus' sense of mission under two comprehensive categories. In Part II, Jesus appears as an eschatological prophet who engaged in controversial behavior and proclaimed the kingdom of God in stories. Part III, The Aims and Beliefs of Jesus, claims that Jesus interpreted his mission messianically and gave a redemptive interpretation of his coming death. The outline broadly resembles that of Jeremias. In Part IV Wright draws out his concluding results.

G. B. Caird

G. B. Caird died in 1984 with a manuscript on New Testament theology less than half finished. Shortly thereafter L. D. Hurst undertook the task of editing and completing the work in a way that would approximate Caird's intentions as closely as possible: *New Testament Theology* (1995). (In referring to this book I will use only Caird's name.)

In chapter 1 Caird lays out his method and approach for writing a New Testament theology. His intention is to be descriptively historical. The category that defines the primary units that structure the work, however, is theological. The single theme that presides over the development of the book is salvation, and chapters 2 through 8 deal with different aspects of that theme: the overall plan, the need of salvation, the three tenses of salvation, the fact of salvation (revelation and atonement), the experience of salvation, the hope of salvation, and the bringer of salvation. Chapter 9 then discusses the theology of the historical Jesus, which is taken very much to be the starting point and goal of New Testament theology. Chapter 10 presents a summary of the findings, and the Epilogue deals very briefly with some hermeneutical issues pertaining to meaning and authority.

While, as we have seen, the defining units of the organization are theological, within each of chapters 2 through 8 Caird sees himself as conducting an apostolic conference or directing a dialogue among the several New Testament witnesses, allowing the New Testament witnesses to speak for themselves on the issue under discussion. This is essentially a comparative historical method (1995:1, 2, 22, 409).

Walter Schmithals

In his *Theology of the First Christians* (German ed. 1994; English trans. 1997), Walter Schmithals intends to write an objective history of early Christian theology. But he recognizes that the tradition is fragmentary in nature and that, therefore, no comprehensive, totalizing history can be written. Rather he discusses eighteen individual topics, of which, while they build on each other, each is a whole unit complete and understandable in itself (1997:ix–xi). The topics range across general theological issues: Paul's conversion theology, Christology, soteriology, church, sacraments, ethics, and so forth. Schmithals begins with a question about the historical Jesus (his relationship to apocalyptic) and ends with a discussion of the formation of the New Testament canon. He denies—at least tacitly—that the historical Jesus properly belongs within the scope of New Testament theology (12, 15; a reaffirmation of Bultmann), but maintains the authority of the canon (369).

While Schmithals intends to give a strongly historical account of New Testament theology, the units that give structure to his project have theological titles. We note, for example: Jesus and the Son of Man, Kingdom of God and Kingdom of Christ, Paul's Theological Development, and Worship in Early Christianity. These themes are closer to the New Testament than to the categories of systematic theology, and each theme is treated in its historical context. Although the topic is theological, the subtopics often show how that theme or phenomenon was treated in different historical settings or how it unfolded historically, for example: Worship in Early Christianity—The Palestinian Church; The Universalist Damascene Churches; The Hellenistic Jewish Christian Churches; Pauline Gentile Christianity; The "Early Catholic" Churches; Pliny's Letter to Emperor Trajan; The Didache; and Justin Martyr. On the other hand, the subthemes may be theological, or primarily so, and deal with different aspects of the main topic, for example: Paul's Conversion Theology—Gnostic Language and Ideas in Paul; Preexistence Theology; Stratifications in Paul's Theology; Observations on Paul's Conversion; and The Origins of Paul's Conversion Theology.

Georg Strecker

When Georg Strecker died in 1994 he left an almost finished set of manuscripts and cassettes for a New Testament theology, which were completed and edited by Friedrich Horn: *Theology of the New Testament* (German ed. 1996; English trans. 2000). Strecker chooses to outline his work from a chronological point of view. This means beginning with Paul, both because Paul's writings are the oldest in the New Testament and because Paul is the only New Testament writer to have implied a systematic theological system. This is important for assessing the later effects of the New Testament writings (Strecker 2000:10–11).

We may not presuppose a single unified theology of the New Testament, for we are met with a multitude of theological conceptions. Each of these is to be investigated in the light of its own thought structure and its historical and literary context. There will be special attention given to the way in which "redactors" used and reinterpreted traditions that came to them. This work will not be a history of early Christian religion or theology, as if a straight line could be drawn from the earliest to the latest stages. The emphasis will not so much be on development as on the theological conceptions of the several New Testament authors (Strecker 2000:2–3).

The order of the topics is, nevertheless, roughly chronological, and each primary structuring unit has a title that names an author or a group of authors or related materials, and also usually expresses a theological theme. There are six major units: (1) Redemption and Liberation—The Theology of Paul; (2) Early Christian Tradition to the Composition of the Gospels; (3) The Way of Jesus Christ—The Synoptic Gospels; (4) Truth and Love—The Johannine School; (5) On the Way to the Early Catholic Church—The Deuteropauline Literature; and (6) A Message with a Universal Claim—The Catholic Letters. The subtopics and sub-subtopics are most often theological themes. Those that receive the primary attention are Christ, the church, and eschatology.

Variations

Whether or not Christology is the main content of the New Testament, as Ernst Käsemann, for example, declares (1973:239, 244), it is certainly extremely important. Works that treat the New Testament interpretation of Christ comprehensively, therefore, suggest further variations on the relationship of historical to thematic categories.

In Oscar Cullmann's *The Christology of the New Testament* (second German ed. 1958; English trans. 1959) the primary structural headings refer to different temporal aspects of the work of Jesus—earthly, future, present, and preexistent. The subtopics are the various christological titles, and each of these is treated in terms of its historical development. For example, under the future work of Jesus, Cullmann discusses Messiah and Son of Man and traces the development of each from Judaism through Jesus to the early church.

Reginald H. Fuller, in his *The Foundations of New Testament Christology* (1965), takes various religion-historical contexts as his primary structural units. First, he deals with the sources or tools (titles) of Christology in Palestinian Judaism, Hellenistic Judaism, and Gentile religion. Then comes a chapter on the self-understanding of the historical Jesus, followed by three chapters on the employment of the tools in the preaching of the earliest church, the Hellenistic Jewish mission, and the Gentile mission. Most of the subtopics of these discussions are the various christological titles, as he shows how these were employed and interpreted in the different religion-historical settings.

Ferdinand Hahn's *The Titles of Jesus in Christology* (German ed. 1963; English trans. 1969) rather reverses Fuller's ordering of primary and secondary headings. Hahn's primary structuring units are the titles themselves—Son of Man, Kyrios (Lord), Christ, Son of David, and Son of God—and the subtopics are the different settings or texts in which these titles are used—the Old Testament, Judaism, Hellenism, Gentile Christianity, and so forth—or they deal with some aspect of the title's meaning—the passion and resurrection of the Son of Man or the exaltation and future coming of the Son of Man, for example.

It is evident that these three books, as well as many other works, present New Testament Christology in large part as an interpretation of the titles. In 1986 Leander E. Keck published a provocative article in which he asserted that while the christological titles and the tracing of their historical development are important, the recent "preoccupation" with them has led to a distortion of the Christology of the New Testament. What is needed is a genuinely theological approach that attends to christological material in addition to the titles and that systematically displays Jesus' relationship to God, the creation, and the human condition (1986:362–63, 368, 370).

Whether the connection between Keck's article and Marinus de Jonge's *Christology in Context* (1988) is causal or coincidental, the structure of the latter work reflects Keck's call to marginalize somewhat the role of christological titles. De Jonge's intention is to portray the historical development of New Testament Christology from the earliest traditions to the Johannine literature. The primary structuring units are texts or groups of texts: Mark, Paul, the Pauline School, etc. Following the historical survey there are three chapters that discuss theological themes that various texts use to interpret the early church's response to Jesus: (1) Jesus as

Herald of the New Age; (2) Jesus' Death, Resurrections, and Exaltation; and (3) Jesus' Preexistence with God. The very last chapter argues back to the historical Jesus and finds him to have had a messianic self-understanding. The subtopics of the chapters can be historical references, theological themes, or christological titles.

De Jonge's project is to set forth the New Testament's varying interpretive responses to Jesus in the light of the life contexts provided by both the cultural-religious situations and the self-understandings of the Christian communities. He is more interested in problems of belief than in titles (16–18), but his goal is historical understanding, not hermeneutical guidance for modern Christology (214).

Frank J. Matera's *New Testament Christology* (1999) also displays a move away from the "preoccupation" with christological titles. While Matera does not neglect the titles, he relativizes their importance and focuses on Jesus' relationships (2–3, 47). The insightful final chapter summarizes the various New Testament writers' positions on Jesus' relationships to Israel, the nations, the church, the world, the human condition, and God. The prominence of these themes lends to New Testament Christology a significant unity, but diversity is seen in the distinctive ways in which different writers develop the themes. Matera does not allow that the diversity amounts to outright contradictions. Rather, the genius of the canon is its ability to hold unity and diversity together in creative tension (1–2, 255).

Matera's project is not to trace the precanonical history of the christological titles but to set forth the Christology embedded in the New Testament itself. This entails not treating the historical Jesus. While Matera is tacitly interested in articulating the historical sense of New Testament Christology, his method employs a literary approach that centers upon the significance of narrative for interpreting who Jesus is. His discussions of the Christologies of the Gospels tend to the paraphrastic summaries of the narratives. One of the most interesting aspects of the book, however, is Matera's teasing out of the implied narratives that underlie the Christologies of the epistles.

The primary structuring units of the book are theological themes, and the subtopics are the New Testament texts that manifest these themes. For example, we have Crucified Messiah and Obedient Son of God: Mark and Matthew; The Climax of Israel's Story: Paul's Letters; and Victory through Suffering: 1 Peter, Hebrews, Revelation.

Perhaps the most unfulfilled element in Matera's study is his hope that the work will enrich and contribute to the systematic study of Christology (4). He may have established a point of departure, but he has not begun to build a bridge to contemporary Christology. Matera discusses the virginal conception of Jesus, his miracles, his resurrection and exaltation, his second coming, and the incarnation of the preexistent Son and Word in the appropriate contexts; but he seems to take all of these theological claims at face value. He gives no indication that these christological motifs pose a problem for contemporary constructive Christology. He does not try to make sense of them or "naturalize" them to current worldviews. Matera does not raise the question about what the language of the motifs could actually refer to in the discourse of our time. All of these issues are related to the presence of mythological language in the New Testament, which all too much contemporary scholarship ignores as if it were not a problem.

The works discussed above represent several distinctive ways of organizing New Testament theology or Christology. In order to recall the variety expressed, I mention selectively several configurations abstracted summarily and schematically from the works just considered:

1. primary structuring units in the form of *historical* persons, texts, or history-of-religions settings, placed in a largely chronological unfolding, with secondary units being historical, theological, or both;

2. scheme #1 preceded by extensive hermeneutical and contextual discussions;

3. scheme #1 sandwiched between discussions of related constructive theological issues;

4. primary organizing units in the form of *theological* categories—relatively loosely, or closely, related—developed in subtopics that are theological, historical, or both;
5. primary structural units as aspects of a single *theological* theme that governs and unifies the whole work, developed by theological subtopics.

3

New Testament Theology: Extra-textual or Textual?

New Testament Theology as Extra-textual

For many scholars New Testament theology is concerned with something outside of the text. In this mode the text becomes the access to the real subject matter of New Testament theology. It has been characteristic for New Testament theologians to look through the text at various aspects of history, which for them is the external object of their interpretations. In this chapter, I will simply look at three examples of the fact of the historical pursuit, while in chapter 4 more attention will be given to the motivations and results of a strictly historical approach.

For William Wrede the proper subject matter of New Testament theology is the history of early Christian religion and theology—what was taught, believed, hoped for, striven for in the historical process itself—not the New Testament writings (84–85).

Oscar Cullmann's New Testament theology focuses on the content and significance of the mission of the historical Jesus. But Jesus is seen as the midpoint and center of meaning of a connected series of real, datable historical events in which God reveals God's self. Wrede's New Testament theology deals with the historical unfolding of the early Christian religion. Cullmann's deals with a succession of revelatory events (1959:8, 316–18, 327; 1967:15, 186–291, 294, 298).

For Joachim Jeremias, more exclusively than with Cullmann, the theological interpretation of the New Testament centers upon the historical Jesus (1963: Foreword; 1964:12–15).

In none of these cases is the New Testament itself the primary object of attention. The focus on some aspect of history outside the New Testament entails certain hermeneutical presuppositions. (1) The text is valuable as a source of knowledge of something more valuable that lies outside of itself. (2) The text is to be looked *through* rather that *at* or *into*. (3) Meaning is found in the relationship between the text and what it refers to with the emphasis on the latter. (4) The language of the text is functioning in a primarily referential way.

Finally, I note a possible non-historical type of outside reference. According to Brevard S. Childs, Bultmann's existential level of interpretation, his interpretation of faith as self-understanding and authentic existence, is a content that lies outside or behind the text (Childs 1970:102). James M. Robinson, however, has argued convincingly that Bultmann tracked down a level of meaning beneath the conscious level of the text and interpreted that meaning in existential terms so that the new terminology actually brings the subject matter of the text to expression. Thus, while Bultmann's existential understanding is not on the surface of the text, it is nevertheless latent in the text rather than being an intrusion from outside (Robinson 1976:20).

New Testament Theology as Textual

Four examples will illustrate the position that the text of the New Testament is the proper subject matter of New Testament theology.

Bultmann may not have given focal attention to this particular question, but there is a tendency in his thought to say that theological meaning is in the word rather than in something behind the word. For example, he maintains that if Jesus did not really speak the words attributed to him, that would not diminish the significance of the record itself (1958a:14). This thought is extended into Bultmann's high evaluation of the proclaimed word as saving event (1951:302–5; 1958b:64, 71, 78–79) and his understanding of New Testament theology as setting forth the theological thoughts of the New Testament writings (1955a:237; 1960a:2).

It turns out that the New Testament texts that elicit Bultmann's own theological voice and that function as his canon within the canon are Paul and John. These two writers grasp most clearly the kerygmatic norm that the saving event was both historical and eschatological (1955a:116–17, 122–27).

Why do the Synoptic Gospels fall outside of Bultmann's canon within the canon? Bultmann believes that it is the very phenomenon of a continuous chronological-geographical narrative that undermines the paradoxical simultaneity of history and eschatology in the representation of the saving occurrence. This is especially the case with Luke, but the danger is also present in Mark and Matthew (1955a:116–17, 122–27). Somehow the Synoptic Gospels do not have a fully adequate understanding of Christian existence, and Bultmann does not regard them as amenable to an existential interpretation that could manifest their pertinence for today.

Since for Bultmann it is precisely the extended narrative that threatens the union of history and eschatology, he must be presupposing that it is only in a moment or point of time that they can be rightly connected. This point of time can be seen in Paul in that he proclaims the death and resurrection of Jesus and their significance without any detailing of historical events (Rom 4:23-25; 1 Cor 15:3-11; 2 Cor 5:18-19; 8:9; Phil 2:6-11). And the temporal point can be seen in John in that he reduces the revelation of God in Jesus to the mere fact that Jesus calls attention to himself as the Revealer (1955a:41, 62–63, 123, 127). Of course, John, like the Synoptics, is a narrative, and I have tried to suggest elsewhere (Via 1997:185) how Bultmann might have been able to see John's narrative as one extended moment.

Thus it would seem that for Bultmann the definitive and normative sphere of Christian existence is the moment when one makes the decision to change one's understanding of human existence. Faith tends to be absorbed in that point of time when one responds to the crisis moment created by the proclamation of Jesus' death and resurrection. Or the life of faith is a series of more or less detached moments (Bultmann 1951:300, 303; 1962b:149–55; 1962a:183).

In response to Bultmann several points should be made. The Synoptic narratives image the life of faith with a concreteness that enhances the power of the language of the gospel. This concreteness is needed to balance the relative generality and abstractness of the proclamation of Jesus' death and resurrection. Because these narratives have palpable shape or form, they address the shaped or embodied nature of human existence in a more complete way than a more conceptual language does. It is not at all self-evident that the Synoptic Gospels are not amenable to existential interpretation. The point is that the existential implications are different from the ones that Bultmann derives from Paul and John. For the Synoptic narratives existence in faith is not a moment-like response to a single crisis. It is rather story-like. It is an ongoing movement through an extended story that contains both continuities and discontinuities.

In *The Ethics of Mark's Gospel* I sought to demonstrate the significance of that Gospel's specifically narrative character for the hermeneutical appropriation of the Markan theology and ethics.

Brevard S. Childs is in agreement with Bultmann on the basic point that the subject matter of New Testament theology should be the New Testament itself. But he also disagrees with Bultmann in certain significant ways, of which I will mention two. For Childs the canon—the *whole* canon and *nothing but* the canon—is the proper context for theological interpretation. This means that he rejects Bultmann's existential interpretation on the ground that it injects an outside or extra-canonical vantage point into the discussion; but I suggested above that this is not a convincing criticism. Childs also rejects the legitimacy of a canon within the canon and hence would be critical of Bultmann's favoring of Paul and John (1970:102; 1984:28, 30, 38, 40, 42, 48, 52–53).

Childs's exegetical practice does not remain strictly within the canon, nor does he escape at least implying a canon within the canon. This is displayed in the way that he deals with an obvious tension in the Gospels. The Synoptic Gospels identify John the Baptist with Elijah (Mark 1:3; Matt 3:4; 17:11-13; Luke 3:4) and thus imply that John is an eschatological figure alongside Jesus. The Gospel of John denies that dignity to John the Baptist (1:21). How is the conflict to be resolved?

Childs states that the Gospels are not to be read on the same level, but rather the Fourth Gospel is the framework from which to interpret the Synoptics (1984:170–73). But he has elsewhere explicitly denied that the Fourth Gospel is the framework for or that it is more authoritative than the other Gospels (1984:153–55). However, as we see, one side of his discussion attributes a higher authority to the Gospel of John (1984:170–73). This assigning of different levels of authority to different books implies a canon within the canon. Some are more authoritative than others. And the *choice* to assign priority to John takes Childs out of a strictly canonical framework. Nothing in the canon itself directs him to prioritize John. His preference for John is derived from *his interpretation* of the canon, which is shaped by his whole life situation.

According to A. K. M. Adam, New Testament theology should be genuine theological discourse and clearly distinguishable from the history of the early Christian religion. It might be expected to concentrate on the writings of the New Testament itself and not on noncanonical works like the Apostolic Fathers or the Gospel of Thomas nor on hypothetical documents such as the Q source (1995a:182–83). At the same time the New Testament should not be seen as a *container* of sense, but as a site to which the interpreter can *ascribe* sense in the light of his or her imaginative deployment of his or her own categories (1995a:170–71; further discussed in chapter 6 below).

For G. B. Caird the task of New Testament theology is to describe what the various writers believed in. While he wants to involve all of these writers in a dialogue or colloquium, the canonical principle per se does not have the programmatic intensity that it has in Childs (Caird 1995:4, 18, 20, 22, 409). While Caird does not appeal to a history outside of the New Testament itself, it is unclear whether his real interest is the writings or the writers of the New Testament.

4

New Testament Theology
as a Historical Project

Scholars who seek to understand the theology of the New Testament rigorously in the light of its first-century context do so for different reasons and in diverse ways. I will deal with several of these scholars under two headings and then look at two central theological themes.

The Historical Pursuit in the Interest of
Objective Knowledge

William Wrede

Wrede called for a New Testament theology that is strictly historical and objective, carried on without regard for the doctrine of inspiration and not limited to canonical sources. The historian need not be influenced by his or her own contemporary viewpoint and should not be concerned to serve the interests of the church or systematic theology; that would be an untenable breach of objectivity. Wrede was interested in historical knowledge for its own sake. New Testament theology, like every area of research, has its goal in itself and must be guided by a disinterested concern for knowledge (1973:69–70, 72–73, 84–85, 101, 116).

Wrede stated in a classical way the ideal of objective historiography that has governed so much twentieth-century New Testament scholarship. However, we should note some tension in Wrede's position. How can scholars distinguish the essential from the secondary—as Wrede says they should (77, 81)—if the scholar's subjective set of values does not make some contribution to the analysis? Moreover, Wrede declares that the scholar should demonstrate order and development in the history of early Christianity and not merely produce a succession of events, experiences, and beliefs (92, 95). But Wrede also acknowledges the very fragmentary nature of the historical evidence (98). How can the scholar bring order and development out of fragments apart from some employment of the imagination and literary construction?

We should recall that Walter Schmithals, acknowledging the fragmentary nature of the sources, gives up the effort to write a comprehensive, developmental history of early Christian theology and instead deals with limited, relatively discrete topics.

It is worth nothing that Helmut Koester's *Introduction to the New Testament*, vol. 2 (1983), while not called a New Testament theology, comes close to fulfilling Wrede's prescription for that genre. This *Introduction* does not *focus* on the scholarship, date, integrity, and literary structure of each New Testament writing but does, nevertheless, deal with these topics in the course of reconstructing the historical development of early Christianity. For this historical purpose Koester regards noncanonical texts as no less valuable than the New Testament (xix).

Krister Stendahl

Stendahl, in his now classic article, "Biblical Theology, Contemporary" (1962), gave currency to the distinction between "what it meant" and "what it means." He comes out strongly for the position that the task of biblical theology is a descriptive rendering of what the biblical texts originally meant. He suggests that the full theological task has three stages: (1) a description of the original historical meaning; (2) clarification of hermeneutical principles; and (3) a probing of the meaning here and now. But biblical theology is virtually limited to the first of these stages. Stendahl nods at the fact that total objectivity is not possible but hastens on to assure us that almost complete objectivity is within our grasp. Objective description is the task of biblical theology; the meaning for the present is not involved (1962:418, 420, 422).

Stendahl does go on to allow that descriptive biblical theology has a right to pass tentative and relative judgments on the various ways in which systematic theology has stated the meaning of the Bible for the present (1962:427). But in a slightly later article,

Stendahl seems to constrict that tentative right. Only systematic theology can decide whether it has properly translated the biblical intention; only systematic theology can deal adequately with the normative question of what it means. The biblical scholar is usually lacking in the requisite theological and philosophical knowledge (1965:199, 202, 204–5).

In a more recent article Stendahl basically reaffirms his distinction between "what it meant" and "what it means" and his definition of biblical theology as a quest for objective description of what it meant. He does acknowledge that description is more imaginative and creative than he had thought, but biblical theology is still concerned with such "original" meanings as what Paul intended and what his readers heard (2000:61–63). Stendahl recognizes that the Bible needs to be interpreted in and for the ever-changing situations in which it is read, but that is part of the task of systematic, not biblical, theology (63).

At the beginning of chapter 5, I argue that in principle a hermeneutical component—what it means—is integral to the task of New Testament theology. Stendahl's denial of that claim artificially restricts the scope of the discipline. Moreover, if the biblical scholar may be lacking in theological and philosophical knowledge to deal with what it means, the systematic theologian may not have the historical and linguistic tools to know what it meant. How then can he or she assess the adequacy of the hermeneutical translation?

Heikki Räisänen

In *Beyond New Testament Theology* (1990), Räisänen praises the historical goals of Wrede but has his own nuances. He believes that New Testament theology has been dominated by theological concerns but should be more historical (63–64, 74, 90). True, complete objectivity is not possible, but a high degree of it can be attained, and a high degree is far superior to a low degree (106). Yet for Räisänen historical knowledge is not for its own sake but paves the way to understanding. It is a question of the roots of our religion and culture (98–99).

A more recent article of Räisänen manifests a change of tone, if not position. He seems to hold that the proper goal of New Testament interpretation is a global relevance, the liberation of all humankind to a life of fullness and justice. But historical criticism is not the enemy of this goal. Räisänen calls for a dialectical interaction between, on the one hand, a historical criticism that aims at relative objectivity and attempts to distinguish between reconstruction (what it meant) and application (what it means) and, on the other hand, various specific liberationist enterprises (Räisänen 2000:9, 11, 13, 23, 25, 27).

Räisänen denies that the great historical critics suffered under the illusion that their objectivity lifted them above the limitations and conditions of their own time (2000:12). Historical criticism can help us distinguish between the historical meanings of texts and their potential for contemporary application. It will enable us to see certain offensive elements in the Bible, for example, that the thirst for vindication in the Apocalypse of John will not contribute to the contemporary struggle for justice (15). Moreover, reading from particular contemporary locations may help give us a new slant on historical meanings. For example, reading from the standpoint of Indian spirituality may show that the Old Testament misunderstood the nature of "idol worship" (19–20).

Burton L. Mack

Burton Mack would doubtless not identify himself as a New Testament theologian; nevertheless, the expansive historical framework that he develops to contextualize Mark's Gospel bears a family resemblance to Wrede's definition of New Testament theology: A Myth of Innocence (1988). In Mack's view, it is not possible for critical scholarship to locate a single, miraculous originating event for Christianity. That effort should be abandoned and replaced with a quest to discover the historical circumstances, intellectual resources, and social motivations that occasioned the early Christians' imagining of the cosmic Christ drama. It is social experience that prompted the imaginative activity, and that is what the New Testament texts are reflective of and upon (6, 8–9,

15, 21). There is no need for recourse to theological categories—such as resurrections, divine appearances and revelation—in order to explain the origin of Christianity (23, 322).

It is true that the emergence of early Christian theology can be accounted for in historical and cultural terms; but the fact that historical interpretation is possible does not mean that theological interpretation is necessarily excluded. Complex phenomena are in principle amenable to more than one level of interpretation. If God is transcendent—hidden—then the disclosure of God will be hidden in the ordinary. Historical criticism can serve the transcendence of God and the hiddenness of revelation by showing that any alleged revelation can be given a completely historical explanation.

Mack faults the guild of New Testament scholars for being taken in by the myth of a miraculous origin of Christianity—the resurrection of Jesus and its euphemistic synonyms. These scholars have generally been unwilling to subject this phenomenon to reasoned argument. This shows that they have in fact been driven by the early Christian imagination. They have not been able to recognize that the miraculous point of origin is not a category of critical scholarship at all, but rather an article of faith derived from Christian mythology (7–8). Mack consistently gives the impression that he, on the other hand, is offering an objective, critical account. Nothing could be further from the truth.

First, it is a fundamental claim of Mack's project that there is no necessary connection between the historical Jesus of the Galilean ministry and the crucified Jesus of Mark's passion narrative. These two Jesuses are too different to have belonged to the same history (10, 56, 355). To this it must be rejoined that such a claim is a theoretical decision regarding identity and difference, a kind of decision that historians regularly and necessarily make, but a type of decision that takes historical investigation out of the realm of the objectively certain and into the tissue of uncertainty that affects other forms of inquiry (see Cousins 1989:127–28).

Second, Mack makes many negative value judgments about early Christianity and Mark in particular. Various constructs in

Mark are referred to as: inauthentic, implausible, dishonest, inappropriate, disastrous, self-serving, vicious, fantastic, rationalizing, bizarre, pitiful, and vindictive (167–71, 198–204, 244–45, 257, 295, 331, 339, 346, 353–57, 376).

Third, the last pages of the book show that this alleged historical-critical work was in considerable part directed all along by a slanted hermeneutic of suspicion, with no balancing hermeneutic for the recovery of meaning. Mark is held responsible for some of the more unfortunate developments in Christianity (356, 362–63) and made culpable for the military interventionism of recent American foreign policy. Mark portrayed Jesus as an innocent redeemer of great power and authority who was rejected and killed. Because he was innocent, he had a right to use his power to punish his enemies (204–6, 355–57). This Markan legacy can be seen in the American sense of innocent power. When others reject our desire to extend the blessings of the American way into their region, we are dismayed and feel that our innocence justifies the use of violence (368, 372–74).

I would not want to argue that there is no truth in Mack's last point. But I would want to object to his monolithically unnuanced interpretation of the Gospel of Mark.

Walter Schmithals

Schmithals stands somewhere between the scholars I have just discussed and those that I am about to review. He intends to do New Testament theology as an objective, historical project (1997:x). But he also holds to the authority of the New Testament (369), although he does not articulate this in the express way that, say, Jeremias, Cullmann, and Caird do.

Schmithals's historical reflections present some interesting and intriguing configurations; however, his dominating methodological tendency has a disintegrative effect. That is, he characteristically traces paragraphs, ideas, motifs, and images back to their presumed source *behind* the text, and he often allows this to prevent him from taking a steady look at coherences *within* the text. For example, one of the conclusions that deeply shapes his studies of Paul is that we can identify several theological strata in Paul's letters that reflect the sources from which they have emanated.

1. Paul was converted to a theology that he had formerly persecuted, a theology that developed from a synthesis of (a) the apocalyptic gospel of Palestinian Jewish Christianity and (b) a Jewish gnosticism. This conversion theology of Paul was also the seedbed of Johannine theology. It may have been associated with the Stephen-Philip group (Acts 6) but probably emerged in Damascus rather than Jerusalem. Paul's conversion theology was characterized by a dualistic vocabulary, freedom from the law, preexistence Christology, and an understanding of salvation oriented to the incarnation of the Redeemer and the nullification of sin's power.

2. The second stratum was the Hellenistic Jewish Christianity that developed in Syria and Cilicia, especially Antioch, which also absorbed the early Palestinian apocalyptic preaching. It was characterized by a Christology of adoption and an understanding of salvation oriented to Jesus' cross and resurrection-exaltation and the forgiveness of sins.

3. The third stratum was Paul's own original ideas, above all the doctrine of justification by faith (Schmithals, 63–71, 75–80, 82, 85–94, 104–19, 132, 135).

I will give two examples of the disintegrative tendency of Schmithals's theological exegesis. Schmithals holds that already in pre-Pauline Hellenistic Jewish Christianity the dialectic of the "already now" and "not yet" of salvation had emerged and had solved in principle the problem of the delay of the parousia (77, 83). This implies that there is a coherent, if paradoxical, interconnection between present and future eschatology. But he can turn around and treat present (Rom 6:1-4) and future (Rom 6:5, 8) salvation as disparate elements on the ground that the former derived from gnostic (76) or mystery religion (99) influence, while the latter issued from apocalyptic Christianity (76, 99).

In discussing 1 Cor 2:6-10a and 2:10b-16 Schmithals has almost nothing to say about what the juxtaposition of those two sections might contribute to Paul's understanding of the relationship between wisdom and Spirit, the nature and functions of the divine Spirit and human spirit, and the possible interrelationship between Spirit and spirit. What does claim his attention is his argument that the two contiguous sections are independent of each other and disunited in both tradition and conceptuality— because 2:6-10a derives from an apocalyptic source and 2:10b-16 from a gnostic one (130–35).

On the other hand, Schmithals's illuminating discussion of Rom 7:18-20—I do not the good I want, but the evil I do not want—demonstrates an organic connection between the position of Epictetus on this idea and Paul's hermeneutical appropriation of the Stoic viewpoint (143–46).

Georg Strecker

Strecker's *Theology of the New Testament* seems to take a strictly historical approach to the task. However, his affirmation of the New Testament's continuing authority is more developed than that of the other scholars discussed in the first part of this chapter, although it is less explicit than that of those to be discussed in part two, which follows. His hermeneutical articulation is more evident than is the case with the other scholars discussed in this chapter but is less evident than those reviewed in the next chapter.

Strecker seeks to interpret the various New Testament texts in the light of their historical context. His intention is to compare the concepts of the New Testament writers with parallels in the non-Christian religious environment and with the earlier Christian traditions that these writers inherited. Such comparisons enhance the distancing of the interpreter from his or her materials that is inherent in the historical-critical method (2000:3, 20–21). Strecker assigns to systematic theology the task of relating theology from the past to the church's present situation (8).

Yet Strecker upholds the authority of the canon and the relevance and authority of the New Testament for the church of today. The church is always under the obligation to ask itself critically whether its present form is in line with the foundational documents (3, 11). To affirm the New Testament's continuing authority without developing a hermeneutic to justify it is a problem I will discuss at the end of my assessment of Caird.

Nevertheless, Strecker's historical interpretations often bring the present existential significance of the texts (for example—116, 125–27, 134–37, 142–43, 155, 176–78, 261, 351–52) closer to the surface than is the case with, say, Dunn, Caird, and Schmithals. Note, for instance, his discussion of Romans 7 under the title "The 'I' in Conflict" (134–37). And Strecker often relates the New Testament materials to broader theological and philosophical issues.

The significance of the historical Jesus for Strecker's New Testament theology is somewhat ambiguous. On the one hand, he states that the significance of Jesus for faith becomes visible only in the light of the resurrection (252). This seems to mean that the historical Jesus tradition has no independent existential-theological import of its own. The historical Jesus is discussed as a part of the pre-Synoptic tradition; and in a book of some seven hundred pages the content of Jesus' teaching is accorded only ten. On the other hand, Strecker holds that a reconstruction of Jesus' first-century message could prepare the way for a theological model significant for contemporary faith (253). But what this might mean, beyond a passing reference to Jesus' radicality and uniqueness (262), is not made clear.

Strecker's book is an excellent and comprehensive resource, although it does not engage the literary-critical and political and liberationist hermeneutics that have achieved provocative articulation in recent decades.

The Historical Pursuit in Support of Theological Claims

Joachim Jeremias

The primary object of Joachim Jeremias's historical quest is the pre-resurrection, pre-kerygmatic Jesus of history. It matters what Jesus did and taught (1964:12–15; 1971:276–99) because only the Son of Man and his words can invest our message with full authority (1963: Foreword). Jeremias's historical pursuit is a quest for theological authority.

Oscar Cullmann

Cullmann concerns himself with a series of historical events that stretch from Israel's past toward the eschatological future. While these events for Cullmann are where God reveals God's self, they are also real, datable events. Cullmann's attention to the historical Jesus at the center of these events shows that he uses historical reasoning both to constitute and to legitimate revelation (1959:8, 316–18, 327).

The positions of Jeremias and Cullmann raise some questions that should be briefly addressed. If historical criticism is used to establish the historical Jesus as the authoritative content of revelation, as Jeremias proposes, and given the fact that there are many pictures of the historical Jesus contending for our allegiance, where does authoritative revelation lie? Jeremias has tacitly conceded that each historical Jesus is in fact an interpretation of the evidence when he attaches the adjectives "dubious," "subjective," and "hypothetical" to historical knowledge (1964:13–15). Does the revelation then reside altogether in the history of Jesus or also in part in the subjectivity of the scholar's interpretation?

For Cullmann the only justifying reason for the church—in the first century or now—to believe in Jesus as the Messiah is that the historical Jesus believed it about himself (1959:8). This creates for Cullmann an unattractive set of alternatives. If he remains a believer, he must allow his faith to constrain his historical reasoning to find a historical Jesus in the Gospels who believes that he is the Messiah. On the other hand, if his historical investigation leads him to the conclusion that Jesus did not believe that he was the Messiah, Cullmann must renounce his faith for having no basis.

G. B. Caird

Caird employs a historical method to determine what the New Testament writers meant in their original context (1995:1, 3, 18, 20, 409). And although he does not make the constitution and legitimation of revelation the direct intention of his historical work in the way that Jeremias and Cullmann do, he affirms the authority of the New Testament for the church of today (25). The

New Testament is a final revelation, valid for all ages and thus potentially relevant for today (1, 2, 4, 22, 421–2). The combination of a strictly historical (non-hermeneutical) approach to New Testament theology with a claim about the authority of the New Testament is seen in several of the scholars already mentioned and also in others, for example, Dunn. This combination creates an ambiguity that can be displayed by a further look at Caird.

Despite Caird's insistence on descriptive history, he does grant that the historian is constructing the past in light of his or her own present (3, 4). So what about objectivity? And although Caird denies that it is part of the task of New Testament theology to give support to contemporary systematic theology or apologetics (1), he does engage in some insightful theological reflection on the basis of the New Testament (414, 421). In fact, there are points where theology seems to dominate historical interpretation. For example, he apparently takes a theological belief, belief in the Incarnation, as a basis for the proper employment of historical criticism. The latter should not be used to blunt the quest for the historical Jesus. The assumption seems to be that historical criticism *should* identify a historical Jesus whose view of his mission closely approximates in theological terms the Christ that the church has always preached (423–24). That this is his assumption is borne out by the fact that his interpretation of Jesus yields a highly messianic historical Jesus (346–49, 404–8).

For Caird, the intention of the biblical authors is the criterion for descriptive, historical interpretation (21, 25, 422–23). This has been such a widely held view among historical interpreters of the Bible that it should be addressed. Most types of literary-critical thinking have renounced the subjective intention of the author as the touchstone of accurate interpretation. The author's intention is never directly and fully available because whatever he or she intended to say, it would have been somewhat reshaped by the palpability of a natural language that already had meanings conferred upon it by general, social usage. Moreover, the more poetic a text becomes—by means of plot, metaphor, irony, parallelism, etc.—the self-referentiality of the poetic language obscures—but does not destroy—any reference to the social context or the author's subjective intention (Jacobson 1972:90, 93, 95–96, 112). It is the text itself that is the proper object of interpretation. Although Caird might seem to direct his attention to the New Testament writings, it is really the thoughts of the writers that are the (unavailable) subject matter of New Testament theology for him.

And even if the author's intention were available, there is a question about whether it would be fruitful. If, hypothetically speaking, the author's intention could be discovered and it agreed with what he or she said in the text, then knowing the intention would be superfluous. If, on the other hand, the hypothetical intention was not in accord with what actually got said, it would not help us to interpret the text we have. All of this is not to say that there are no conditions under which the intention of an author in some part might be discovered. But the effort is too problematical to be at the center of interpretation.

Caird actually goes beyond simply affirming the general principle that the author's intention should be the criterion of correct interpretation and claims a uniqueness for Christianity. According to Caird, Christianity is different from all other religions and philosophies in being a gospel. That is, it is good news about historical events, attested by reliable witness, and centering in a historical person. This means that Scripture is not to be given meanings other than the plain sense intended by the writers (422–23).

Caird's claim is seriously challenged by Frank Kermode's argument that the guild of interpreters has long shown a preference for the latent sense over the manifest and that early Christian writers contributed to this by reading unintended, unhistorical, Christian meanings into the Old Testament (1979:x–xi, 1–2, 18–19). Caird's position ignores the assertion of the Markan Jesus that he teaches in parables in order to frustrate a plain sense (Mark 4:10-12), and it overlooks the fact that the Gospel writers reinterpreted the Jesus tradition for their new situation rather than looking for the original sense.

Despite certain slight tendencies in Caird that reveal his own contemporary theological concerns, he not only omits the development of a hermeneutical component in his New Testament theology, but argues against the approach. It is evident that he fears that hermeneutics will distort the intended meaning, and he disparages the hermeneutical endeavor as "abstruse," "recondite," and "grandiloquent." In Caird's view, the attempt to merge historical clarification with hermeneutical application will almost certainly result in falsity (21–22, 422–23).

Those scholars who understand New Testament theology as a strictly historical project but also maintain the authority of the New Testament for the continuing life of the church over the centuries create a two-part configuration that lacks a connector. The anomaly of their position is that, given their historical approach, they do not develop a hermeneutical vocabulary and conceptuality to represent the theological meanings of the New Testament in such a way that these meanings could address the present moment as a summons that could or should be listened to as compelling and authoritative. That is, the claim of authority is not supported by hermeneutical-theological discourse, a discourse that would demonstrate why the New Testament message should be grasped as taking priority over other understandings of reality today.

Peter Balla

In *Challenges to New Testament Theology* (1997), Balla takes a position similar to Caird's but with its own variations. For Balla, New Testament theology is definitely a *theological* endeavor distinguishable from the history of early Christian religion (contra Wrede). Theology should be understood not just as doctrine, but broadly as all affirmations, actions, and experiences related to the early Christians' belief in God (20–22, 36, 46, 148, 213–14). It is at the same time a descriptive, historical discipline that "has to make use of the methods of historical criticism" in setting forth the theology contained in the New Testament writings in their own context (1–4, 6, 16, 20, 29, 31, 46, 211–15, 232–33, 236, 238). New Testament theology is not normative (32–33, 214). Neither is it a hermeneutical project to actualize the meaning of the New Testament for the present (6, 29, 78, 214, 236, 249).

At first sight Balla's attitude toward hermeneutics seems to be less antagonistic then Caird's. A hermeneutical thrust in New Testament theology is a legitimate possibility, though it is not an inherent or necessary part of the discipline and not an option that Balla chooses to pursue. There is no definite answer to the question about the character of New Testament theology but rather a plurality of supportable possibilities (240, 250).

However, as Balla's position unfolds, it seems to become less neutral and more negative and prescriptive. He is afraid that if the interpreter moves beyond what the historian as descriptive historian can say, then interpretation will get out of control and produce results that are implausible and improbable (233, 236). He also assumes that New Testament theology in the hermeneutical mode necessarily entails the scholar's attempt to convince readers that they should accept the truth claims of the New Testament (236, 245, 250).

To these contentions I have three responses: (1) Historical investigation does not give the kind of objectivity that Balla seems to assume but hangs with other forms of inquiry in a tissue of uncertainty (Cousins 1989:127–28). (2) Hermeneutics need not lead to the arbitrary or implausible. The delicate and difficult task of New Testament theology as hermeneutical is to discover a dimension in the New Testament text from the past that can be extended into something new in the present without completely obliterating its continuity with its past. (3) The hermeneutical move need not entail the effort of the scholar to convince readers that they *should* accept his or her interpretation. It is enough that the interpretation be articulated as something that one *could* accept in the present with intellectual honesty. But Balla maintains that the New Testament theologians should renounce *relevance* for the present as well as advocacy (249).

Although Balla disavows the view that New Testament theology is a normative discipline that should advocate a certain interpretation, there is a configuration of motifs that he pursues with such emphasis as to suggest a tacit claim on his part that these things should be believed.

To begin with, he holds that one can argue on *historical* grounds, and not just on dogmatic ones, that New Testament theology should confine itself to the canonical books. His first point is that through a historical process a particular segment of Christianity found its identity defined in just these books. That is a historical datum. The second point is that the New Testament writers themselves, or at least some of them, believed that they were writing canonical or authoritative documents (47, 49, 56, 67, 77, 84–86, 89, 100–1, 109, 113–16, 121, 125–26, 135, 223). Since New Testament theology is to present the theology of the New Testament.itself, this strong emphasis on the New Testament's own sense of authority is an implied claim for the authority of New Testament theology.

For Balla one source of the New Testament's sense of authority is the writers' belief that Jesus was the Messiah (121). Moreover, Balla leans firmly toward the view that Jesus himself had a messianic, if not divine, self-consciousness, although he did not necessarily express this verbally (79, 161, 168, 185). There is no adoptionist Christology in the New Testament (159–65, 179).

Balla conspicuously foregrounds his claim that the theology of the New Testament is a unified position. It is free from development or contradiction (see chapter 2). In Balla's judgment we should understand history in such a way as to be open to the possibility that God does intervene actively in the course of history (16–17, 46). In view of Balla's clear highlighting of this particular configuration it seems not amiss to hold that he makes a tacit claim for the normativity of New Testament theology.

James Barr

The Concept of Biblical Theology (1999) by James Barr also calls for a strongly historical biblical theology without a hermeneutical component. Barr agrees that biblical theology is in some sense really theological, but he takes a curiously ambivalent position toward this issue. He understands real or authentic theology as a reflective activity in which the content of religious expression is to some extent abstracted, contemplated, subjected to discussion, and deliberately reformulated (249).

Most of the Bible itself cannot be understood to *be theology* in this sense. But biblical texts may, nevertheless, be *theological* or contain implicit theology. We could then define the task of contemporary biblical theology as making the implicit theology explicit. Does that then make biblical theology real theology? Well, no (73). Biblical theology—with its concern for language, literary form, environing culture, geography, etc.—is more like exegesis than like theology proper (248–52).

Nevertheless, biblical theology is justified and made unavoidable by the fact that all exegesis of a limited piece of text implies some view of the totality of the text. Biblical theology is a provisional attempt to express that view, whether the totality is the Old Testament, the New Testament, or both together (186, 220).

With minor qualifications Barr holds that Stendahl is basically right. Perfect objectivity is not possible, but the task of biblical theology is to describe as objectively as possible, not so much what the implicit theology in the Bible *meant*, as what it *was*. That is, the job is to describe the *only* meaning the Bible had, which is its *past* meaning. And that is the only meaning it still has (202–4).

Barr, of course, acknowledges that many have understood biblical theology to entail hermeneutics as the effort to interpret or actualize the biblical message for today (15, 379–80). But his critical discussion of this position is skewed from the outset by his repeated insistence on reductionistically categorizing hermeneutics or interpretation for today as faith-committed interpretation (189–91, 198, 204–5, 207). Barr argues that biblical theology does not logically or methodologically require faith commitment on the part of the scholar (15, 191, 194–96, 199, 203–4) and that the faith-commitment position lacks objectivity and commonly fails to set any limits on prejudice, special pleading, or propaganda (205). Interpretation for today is described rather condescendingly as supported by "current popular ideology" (190) and as something to beware of (539, 607).

Barr implies that faith-committed interpretation, existential interpretation, Bultmannian hermeneutics in particular, and postmodernism all belong to the same type of interpretation (147, 149, 205). But this is mistaken. Bultmann, James M. Robinson, John R. Donahue, and Robin Scroggs, for instance, hold that New Testament theology should be hermeneutical but do not believe that one must be committed to the Christian faith in order to give quite satisfactory theological interpretation of the New Testament for today. Bultmann, for example, states explicitly that "correct" interpretation of the New Testament does not require that the interpreter have Christian faith. It does require that he or she have a vital concern about the existential question to which faith is a possible answer (1962a:187). Barr's failure to make appropriate distinctions among different kinds of interpretation for today renders his discussion of hermeneutics beside the point.

Having argued that the Bible has only one meaning—its past meaning—and having argued that interpretations for today are not really interpretations of the *Bible* but of the Bible in the light of other spheres of knowledge (Barr 1999:202–3), Barr then seems to deconstruct that position (204–5). That is, he acknowledges that description of the past entails imaginative construction, the use of modern terms and categories, and comparisons with the way we think. What it meant, therefore, becomes mixed up with what it means for today.

This enlarged view of historical description is quite surprising in view of his strictures against the position that the biblical text can have a meaning for today, that is, any meaning other than its only (past) meaning. He has now actually made the only (past) meaning virtually indistinguishable from the meaning for today claimed by the kind of hermeneutics of which he is so critical.

The interpreters who acknowledge the operation of the hermeneutical circle know that they are interpreting the Bible in light of other spheres of knowledge. But they justly claim that they are in fact interpreting the *Bible,* for they understand that texts have multiple possible meanings—which are based on both the uncertainties and gaps in the text and the multiplicity of hermeneutical questions with which one may approach a text. Barr appears not to know this and thus to claim only one possible legitimate meaning—the past one. But he then deconstructively enlarges that meaning into the very thing he denies—an interpretation of the biblical text *itself* that nevertheless expresses its meaning in contemporary terms, its meaning for today.

Eschatology

Given the stress on the place of eschatology in the New Testament throughout the twentieth century, it is appropriate to mention two important scholars who gave significant attention to this subject. Working to demonstrate the nature of New Testament eschatology in its first-century context, C. H. Dodd and Ernst Käsemann came to divergent conclusions.

C. H. Dodd

In his book on the parables in 1936 (rev. ed. 1961), Dodd maintained the following about the heart of the historical Jesus' proclamation: to the extent that the final and absolute kingly activity of God can occur in history it has already happened in Jesus' historical ministry—hence "realized eschatology." There will be no future coming of the kingdom or Son of Man. Predictions of a future coming are either consciously symbolic or instances of early church tradition (Dodd 1961:viii, 13–19, 29–35, 118–19, 157, 159, 167). Jesus' historical mission *is* the eschatological event. In works both early (*The Apostolic Preaching* [1936]) and late (*The Interpretation of the Fourth Gospel* [1953]), Dodd maintained the centrality of realized eschatology for grasping the meaning of New Testament theology as a whole.

James M. Robinson levels two criticisms against Dodd's position. (1) Anyone who would try to claim that God's reign has already come, that our world is the kingdom of God, deserves to be laughed or cried down. Thus Dodd does not bring the content of the New Testament to expression in a way that is a living and believable alternative for today (1976:18). (2) By portraying the kingdom of God as something visible and manifest in the world, Dodd undermines the risks intrinsic to faith and thus forfeits the New Testament itself (1976:18).

In my judgment neither of these criticisms is justified. Dodd clearly does not think that the kingdom of God has literally transformed the world and made itself unequivocally evident. Rather it is only paradoxically present. Realized eschatology, therefore, neither presents itself as an unbelievable delusion nor undercuts the risk of faith. According to Dodd, the events recorded in the Gospels had little or no immediate or ostensible influence on history. There were no repercussions in imperial affairs and few ripples in Judaism (Dodd 1938:149).

The one incontestable historical result of Jesus' ministry was the emergence of the church. For the New Testament, the rise of the church is a part of the eschatological complex; but the world into which the church came was ostensibly quite unchanged. And the church itself has a paradoxical character. On the one hand, it claims to be a supernatural society—the temple of the Holy Spirit and the body of Christ. On the other hand, it is a community of fallible human beings striving to attain an unrealizable goal in the social, economic, and political structures of the empirical order. The church has never been pure (Dodd 1938:150–53, 156). The eschatological intervention of God in history takes place by means of the proclamation of the Gospel and the sacrament of the Eucharist. It is in these that secular and redemptive history are joined (1938:162–63, 172).

Robinson states that Dodd—and others—have intended to carry on New Testament theology, but what they have actually produced is an antiquated, theologically useless account of what people once thought (1976:18–19). I would judge that probably the opposite is the case. Dodd intended to do historical exegesis, but what he produced is theological interpretation. Dodd should have been more aware than he was of his hermeneutical presuppositions. But his distinguished work in no way deserves the criticisms that Robinson scornfully levels against it.

Interestingly, in considerable part the Jesus Seminar confirms Dodd's analysis of Jesus' teaching about the kingdom of God: It is altogether a matter of realized eschatology (Funk 1993:40, 136–37, 365).

Ernst Käsemann

In the 1960s, Käsemann published two provocative articles on apocalypticism in the New Testament. In the earlier of these, using form-critical methods on the traditions in Matthew, Käsemann found the remnants of two strongly opposed theological positions that he traced back to two groups in earliest Christianity. Although Käsemann's terminology is not always clear and consistent, these two conflicting positions may be called (1) apocalyptic (the Hebrews of Acts 6) and (2) Palestinian apocalyptic enthusiasm (the Hellenists of Acts 6) (1969a:82–89). Each of these positions is defined by four characteristics.

Apocalyptic: (1) The end of the world is imminent (1969a:86, 106). (2) The law of Moses is to be upheld (1969a:85–86, 106). (3) A mission to Israel is to be promoted but not a mission to the Gentiles (1969a:87–88, 106). (4) There is an enthusiasm of imminent expectation (1969a:88, 92).

Palestinian Apocalyptic Enthusiasm: (1) The imminent end is expected (1969a:88). (2) The law of Moses is critiqued or rejected (84–87). (3) A mission to the Gentiles is pursued (87). (4) There is an enthusiasm of present fulfillment (84–88).

These two theological positions differ on points 2 and 3, but both are apocalyptic and both are enthusiastic. Their enthusiasms, however, push in different directions. For Käsemann, enthusiasm seems to mean basically an intense sense of the possession of the Spirit (1969a:88, 92). This gave to Palestinian apocalyptic enthusiasm a conviction about a radically changed present (points 2 and 3). But it gave to apocalyptic a vivid expectation of the imminent eschatological end along with a relatively unchanged present.

Käsemann also identifies a third, slightly later, position that he calls Hellenistic enthusiasm (1969c:124–25). This position rejected not only apocalyptic but any relevant future hope, because it maintained that what apocalyptic hoped for has already been fully realized in the present (1969c:125–26, 130–31). For the Hellenistic enthusiasts, believers have already achieved the goal of salvation. They have been resurrected and enthroned with Christ, liberated from the old age of death and from the cosmic powers, and freed from earthly moral responsibilities and the sway of destiny (1969c:125–26, 129–31). According to Käsemann, this was the position of Paul's theological opponents in the Corinthian church, and traces of it can also be seen, somewhat recontextualized, in the writings of some of Paul's disciples (Eph 2:5; 5:14; Col 2:12-13; Käsemann 1969c:125–26).

According to Käsemann, Paul opposed Hellenistic enthusiasm from an apocalyptic point of view. The end time has broken in, but its completion awaits the future. Believers already share in Christ's death, but their participation in his resurrection is reserved for the eschatological future. Full redemption will not occur until Christ's reign has overcome the hostile cosmic powers and the whole of reality has become subject to God (1 Cor 15:20-28). Paul's interpretation is intended to dispel the illusion of the Hellenistic enthusiasts that salvation is already complete in the present (1969c:125, 131–34, 136–37).

I should now like to point to what appears to me to be three problems or tensions observable in Käsemann's construction of early Christian theology. First, he maintains that apocalyptic was the mother of all Christian theology and that it is the necessary horizon for a proper contemporary theology (1969a:96, 102, 107; 1969c:109–10, 114–15, 137). Thus he makes a very strong positive claim that is both historical and constructive. But Käsemann also asserts that when the resurrected Son of Man failed to return soon in glory, as was expected, the whole theological framework of apocalyptic failed. The future hope, the expected restoration of the twelve tribes of Israel, the championing of the law of Moses, and the rejection of the Gentile mission had all collapsed (1969a:106–7). My question is: How can apocalyptic be the source of all Christian theology and its necessary shaping theme if it collapsed very soon after its inception?

Some light is shed on this puzzle when we recognize that, while Käsemann states programmatically that apocalyptic is the mother of all Christian theology (1969a:102), the development of his argument (not always clear) shows that it is really Palestinian apocalyptic enthusiasm that he regards as the mother of Christian theology. Palestinian apocalyptic enthusiasm affirms both a hope for the near end and also a strong sense of present eschatological fulfillment. While the failure of the near end affects Palestinian apocalyptic enthusiasm as well as apocalyptic, the emphasis on fulfillment in the former offers many possibilities for theological development that do not depend on the expectation of the imminent return of Jesus.

Käsemann's unfolding argument presents Palestinian apocalyptic enthusiasm as the basis for the theology of Paul and John and thus as the real mother of Christian theology. The eschatological significance of the proclaimed word in both Paul and John, the present realization of justification in Paul, and the Johannine affirmation that eternal life and final judgment are present realities all stem from the note of present fulfillment in Palestinian apocalyptic enthusiasm (1969a:102–5).

Second, Käsemann writes as if Paul had fabricated his position from disparate elements in the face of the Corinthian problem. Paul picked up present eschatology from the Hellenistic enthusiasts but limited this by retaining the apocalyptic future hope of the earliest theology (1969c:131–34).

We should note, however, that Käsemann has already attributed both present and future eschatology to the pre-Pauline Palestinian apocalyptic enthusiasm and has argued that Paul's theology developed from that position (1969a:103–5). And Bultmann has shown that the tension between the two eschatological dimensions—present and future—express a single, coherent point of view (see chapter 5).

Third, on the hermeneutical front, Käsemann wants to preserve the public or universal nature of history that belongs to apocalypticism—the course of world history from creation to the eschatological return of the Son of Man, Jesus. Christian theology cannot be adequately interpreted from an existential starting point. Käsemann acknowledges that the apocalyptic worldview is mythological, but he regards it as an unwarranted reduction to interpret apocalyptic as if it applied to the historical existence of the individual. God's future should not be turned into human futurity (1969a:96–97; 1969c:117).

But is it not the case that, just beneath the surface, Käsemann's real interest is apocalypticism's implications about the *understanding* of human historical existence as it pertains to the individual? He states that in the apocalyptic view of history the world is directed to move from a definite beginning through distinguishable epochs to a definite end. This scheme gives to the individual a firmly established place, a particular position in the process (1969a:96–97). Is then the real intentional concern of Käsemann's discussion of apocalyptic history the coming to expression of the particularity of the individual and the banishing of the illusion that salvation can be complete within the course of history? This possibility seems to be supported by the fact that when Käsemann takes up the historical Jesus the move from the historical to the existential becomes more pronounced.

According to Käsemann Jesus was not an apocalypticist; thus the earliest post-resurrection Christian theology made a new theological start when it replaced Jesus' message with apocalyptic (1969a:101–2). The kingdom of God for Jesus was in some sense future (1969c:111, 122), but it was also present (1969c:114, 122). And in fact the future element did not have to do with the chronologically datable end of the world (1969c:112–13). Indeed, Jesus' teaching on the kingdom overcame the customary distinction between present and future. The future defines the present. Jesus proclaimed the immediacy of the near God and thus brought in the eschatological age by announcing it. Jesus' sense of God's immediacy was too great for him to have thought that God's presence had to await the coming of the Son of Man (1969a:101; 1969c:122).

In Käsemann's view Jesus was not a theologian, and his preaching should not be too closely associated with the early church's apocalyptic theology (1969a:102). But New Testament study as a whole must take account of Jesus. And the theological significance of the historical Jesus is set forth in Käsemann's claim that Jesus is the criterion for the legitimacy of all later theological developments (1973:244; 1969b:47–50, 52, 63).

The boundary between Jesus and apocalyptic theology is further diminished by Käsemann's tendency, despite himself, to interpret them both existentially. Although Jesus' proclamation of the future kingdom does not have to do primarily with the end of the world, Jesus still points to a future—one that is characterized by freedom and openness. Jesus is open to God, his fellow human beings, the present moment, and suffering. He becomes Lord by his power to translate others into this freedom that he had (1969c:123–24).

Christology

New Testament theology in recent decades has been attentive to the question about when and in what way Christology began. I will mention two different positions.

One maintains that the historical Jesus had a messianic self-consciousness and interpreted his mission with messianic titles of dignity. Thus a smooth continuity is posited between the historical Jesus and the christological Jesus as the church interpreted him in light of the resurrection. Oscar Cullmann is an obvious example, as are Caird, Wright, and de Jonge.

A second position holds that the historical Jesus did not understand himself in messianic terms and that it was only in consequence of the church's faith in his resurrection that it began to attribute to him such titles as Christ, Son of God, and Lord and the status of preexisting divine being. Thus a discontinuity is posited between the Jesus of history and the Christ of the post-resurrection church. The *proclaimer* of the kingdom of God has become the *proclaimed* Christ whose benefits are affirmed. But the discontinuity is only a relative one because it is also held that the historical Jesus had an implicit Christology. This is seen in his tacit belief that as eschatological prophet he in his own person signified the demand for decision, which he understood as God's last word before the end. This determines the destiny of those who hear. The effect of the resurrection, then, is to turn Jesus' implicit Christology into the church's explicit Christology. This position can be seen, for example, in Rudolf Bultmann (1951:9, 26–32, 42–43; 1969:237, 283) and Reginald H. Fuller (1965:15–16, 103, 130–31, 142–43), though the latter may stress a bit more the continuity between Jesus and the Christian community.

Willi Marxsen

Marxsen is critical of both of these positions. He believes that a definitive decision should not be made for either continuity or discontinuity, for the beginnings of Christology in either the historical Jesus or the Christian community. Rather Christology begins where the relationship between Jesus and the believer becomes visible for the first time (1979:37). Marxsen thinks that this happens in the early tradition that underlies both Luke 12:8-9 and Mark 8:38. Here Jesus is explicitly distinguished from the future Son of Man. The real intent of the passages is not in the future for itself but in proclaiming that one's present relationship with Jesus qualifies one's eschatological destiny (45, 47, 48). Marxsen believes that this motif is very early, but it is difficult to tell whether he would trace it all the way back to the historical Jesus or to a pre-Easter disciple (49, 53–54, 80).

Easter did *not* constitute a significant break in christological development for Marxsen. This is because Jesus is always the one proclaimed, both before and after Easter. That is the continuity in the christological development. Easter did not initiate the transition from proclaimer to proclaimed. Jesus is proclaimed as the proclaimer on both sides of Easter. This means that he is proclaimed as the one who enables faith, brings people to faith. True, after Easter Jesus' functional role of calling people to faith is increasingly portrayed by interpreting his person. Titles are transferred to him such a Son of Man, Son of God, and Christ. This is a change, but the functional role is still primary. A further change occurs when and where Jesus is interpreted, not as the enabler of faith, but as the one believed *in* (66, 67, 78–80, 81–82).

James D. G. Dunn

Finally a more specific question has been raised provocatively by James Dunn: When did Jesus begin to be interpreted as the incarnation of the preexistent Son or Logos (Word)? Dunn acknowledges that the historical Jesus did not believe that he was the incarnation of the preexistent Son of God. And if there were a complete discontinuity between Jesus' own claim and the later doctrine of the incarnation, that would undermine the latter. Dunn maintains, however, that there is continuity. Preexistence is an appropriate reflection on and elaboration of Jesus' view that his intimate filial relationship with God had eschatological significance (1980:23–29, 63, 254).

But Dunn then argues that passages in Paul (Phil 2:5-11) and the Book of Hebrews (Heb 1:1-3), often interpreted as teaching the preexistence of Jesus, are to be read as metaphorical personifications of God's own plan, power, and action and not as references to Jesus' personal preexistence (1980:178, 181–82, 190, 194–95, 209, 211–12, 255–56). The Fourth Gospel is the first and only real witness in the New Testament to Jesus as a personal preexistent being (1980:57–59, 239–41, 243–45, 249).

Why does Dunn deny preexistence to Paul and Hebrews? His ostensible and most sustained argument is that his interpretation is required by the pertinent sources in the Jewish environment of early Christianity. The concept of Jesus' preexistence is, of course, widely held to have been influenced by Jewish categories such as the Word of God or the Wisdom of God (see Mack 1973). Dunn, however, argues that these figures are not divine beings intermediary between God and the world but personifications of God's own functions (1980:168–76). And that is how first-century readers would have understood statements about Jesus influenced by wisdom theology.

Other scholars will read both Paul and Hebrews and the Jewish sources differently from Dunn. It seems especially difficult to me to deny that the divine wisdom in Sirach 24:3-4, 30-31 is a being who came forth from God and then dwelt in heaven with God as a relatively autonomous being.

So let me put the question raised two paragraphs above in different terms. Why does Dunn postpone the emergence of the incarnation of the preexistent Son and Word to a single New Testament document? Dunn is suspicious that the incarnation of the preexistent Son and Word is a mythological construct and a threat to monotheism and that it resulted from a "cultural evolution" influenced by paganism, an evolution that John both drew from and contributed to (1980:248, 253, 262–65). Thus it would appear that Dunn makes the emergence of preexistence in early Christianity as late as possible in order to place it on the outer edge of the New Testament and to marginalize it.

Dunn has a deconstructed view of the development of incarnational Christology in the New Testament. One side of his discussion sees it as a legitimate extension of Jesus' sense of eschatological mission, but the other side sees it as a somewhat foreign distortion.

I should like to propose one possible interpretation of the New Testament incarnational Christology that does justice to the full humanity of the historical Jesus as well as to his mission's eschatological significance and that relates this to the Christian doctrine of the Trinity. This position involves two interpretative claims. (1) To affirm that the Son-Word dimension of God's own transcendent being took up literal, metaphysical residence in the finite, flesh-and-blood existence of the historical Jesus would be a mythological identification of the transcendent with the finite and should be demythologized (see chapter 5). (2) It makes good theological sense to affirm that the personal relationship between the historical Jesus and God (Matt 11:25-27; Mark 1:9-11) is the definitive source of human salvation for Christians and is analogous with, but is not a literal manifestation of, the relationship between Father and Son in the being of God.

In chapter 7 I will try both to give a critique of the objectivist ideal in historical interpretation and to explain why I believe that some type of historical criticism is necessary.

5

New Testament Theology as Historical and Hermeneutical

A hermeneutical component as an integral part of New Testament theology is justified for at least two reasons. (1) The New Testament writers themselves were not focally concerned about what the traditions and sources that they used originally meant, but they rather drew out and constructed from these materials meanings that they adapted and directed to the situations in which they wrote. This I sought to demonstrate in detail in my 1997 book. True, the New Testament writers are often not sufficiently constrained by the original meanings of their traditional material, and in such instances they are not appropriate models for us (1997:71–90). But the hermeneutical task can be carried out in a critically responsible way. (2) If the authority of the New Testament for later times is affirmed, a hermeneutical element is methodologically required. That is, in order to justify the claim of authority it must be shown that the New Testament message(s) can be articulated in such a way as to speak pertinently and forcefully to the present situation.

Rudolf Bultmann

Bultmann combined the historical and hermeneutical in a powerful and perceptive way. This can be seen classically in his descriptions of the historical positions of Paul and John, followed by his interpretations of these two writers, which are imprinted by a twentieth-century philosophy of existence. His programmatic commitment to both of these dimensions can be seen succinctly on the last page of the *Theology of the New Testament*, vol. 2 (1955a). As Robert Morgan has insightfully pointed out, what connects history, philosophy, and theology for Bultmann is their common concern with human existence. The novel thing about Bultmann is that he conceived of the historical dimension of the New Testament in such a way that he could do his theologizing through historical study (Morgan 1973:12, 37–38).

The Hermeneutical Circle Operates in All Interpretation. One must already have a tentative pre-understanding of something in order to understand it at all. Every interpretation is guided by a question, and that question grows out of a life situation that provides the pre-understanding. An interpretation will always incorporate the prior understanding that derives from the context of the interpreter's experience. This means that there is no exegesis without presuppositions. But presuppositions must not determine the outcome of an interpretation. They rather legitimately govern the kind of knowledge or subject matter to be sought (1955b:239–43; 1960b:289, 292–94).

Scope. The scope of the New Testament subject matter with which New Testament theology deals embraces a number of aspects or levels: the historical Jesus—kerygma—faith—theological thoughts (1955a:237–41, 251).

Historical-Critical Method. For Bultmann the historical method is indispensable (1960b:291–92), but it generates two different questions, which seem to be for Bultmann really the only two legitimate questions: (1) What does the text tell me about the past? (2) What understanding of existence does it offer as a possibility for my existence? It is the latter that he pursues (1955a:251; 1955b:235, 246, 253; 1958b:52–53). Language about God, to be authentic, must also be language about human existence.

Demythologizing. This is a dramatic instance of existential interpretation.

1. Bultmann gave three *definitions* of myth and apparently did not discuss the three together in a systematic, synthetic way; nevertheless, there is accord among them. Bultmann's essential and most comprehensive definition of mythological thinking is that it speaks of the divine in human terms, the other side in terms of this side, the transcendent in terms of the finite (1954:10; 1960a:3–4). For example, God's transcendence is

expressed spatially as God's dwelling in the highest place—
heaven. Or God's eternity is expressed chronologically as
beginning at the last moment. Myth occurs when such language is taken literally and God is thereby identified with such
finite categories as time and space and God's transcendence is
undermined. The divine is confused with the earthly (1954:10;
1960a:3).

Myth is also defined by Bultmann as prescientific thinking. This aspect was especially seen by him as manifested in
the three-storied universe—heaven, earth and underworld
(1954:1–8; 1958b:37–38, 83). Space is treated mythologically.
God is spoken of as being in the highest place—heaven—and
Jesus' significance is grounded on his coming from that place.
Thus the transcendent is circumscribed within space. But Bultmann also defined myth as primitive science. It is science in that
it assigns causes to certain events, but it is primitive in that these
causes are otherworldly. God intervenes in historical and natural
processes and thus becomes an object like these processes
(1958b:18–19, 61). If the Holy Spirit literally generated Jesus in
the womb of the virgin Mary, then the Holy Spirit is turned into
a biological agent. If Jesus literally calmed the storm with a
word, then the divine word is indistinguishable from the
weather.

2. For Bultmann the *purpose* of myth is not to give a factual
   description of the universe as it is. It is rather to offer a certain
   understanding of human existence, to portray human beings
   as placed in a world whose origin and purpose are grounded,
   not on the tangible, but on the transcendent reality upon
   which the world is dependent (1954:10–11; 1958b:19; 1960a:2;
   1962a:185).

3. Demythologizing has two moments. The first one is negative,
   acknowledging that the mythological motifs are not literally
   true (1954:4–8). The second one is positive, recovering the
   myth's original understanding of existence and interpreting
   that in a way that is compelling and pertinent in our situation
   (1954:10, 16; 1960a, 2–3). As is well known, Bultmann used

concepts from Martin Heidegger's philosophy of existence to interpret the human situation prior to faith and under faith.

4. The motivation for demythologizing is provisionally apologetic: to make the New Testament message more acceptable to modern people by removing the prescientific ideas that are impediments to faith. These motifs are unbelievable for us and have no essential connection to the gospel anyway (1954:3; 1962a:183). The fundamental motivation for demythologizing, however, is constructive: to support the transcendence of God by showing that myth taken literally undermines that transcendence (1954:11; 1955a:238; 1960a:2–3). This clarifies the nature of faith as a risky decision, for the transcendent God is always present as *hidden*. This God is available only to the eyes of faith and is never an object that is subject to manipulation by human reason or sense perception (1958b:19, 61–62, 84–85; 1962a:183).

5. The value of Bultmann's definition of myth is that it is truly a definition. That is, it delineates or distinguishes myth from other kinds of symbolic language and shows that myth in essence undermines the transcendence of God. Bultmann has often been misunderstood on the issue of his definition of myth and sometimes by the best of scholars. Norman Perrin, for example, insisted that Bultmann consistently interpreted myth as a prescientific cosmology (1976:73, 79), although we have seen that that is only an expression of the more basic definition.

Perrin was right that Bultmann did not grasp the power of symbolic language to have multiple references and levels of meaning (1976:72–80), but Perrin's alternative also creates problems. He accepts a much broader understanding of what myth is than does Bultmann. Myth is a complex of stories—whether fact or fantasy—that human beings regard as demonstrations of the inner meaning of the universe and of human life (22). Contra Perrin when myth is defined so broadly and inclusively, myth in Bultmann's narrower sense tends to be lost sight of—language that literally identifies God with time, space, causality and substance—

and such language, inadequate to the biblical view of God's transcendence, is used in forgetfulness of its inadequacy.

The Individual. Bultmann's interpretation of the New Testament tends to focus on the meaning of human existence for the *individual* person (1955b:235). He is concerned about the historicity of the individual, by which he means that we become ourselves, gain our essence, through the decisions that we make in our encounters with life's experiences. Meaning is not to be found by looking around us at universal history but by looking into our own personal histories (1962b:42–44, 151, 155).

The Christian believer stands paradoxically both above history and also within his or her own historicity, and the specific historicity of the believer is constituted by his or her decision to accept the proclamation of Jesus' death and resurrection. This decision of faith is a decision for a new self-understanding: I renounce the belief that my existence is at my own disposal and understand myself as free from myself by the grace of God and endowed with a new self living into the future. But the decisive event has already happened. The bliss of apocalyptic salvation is attributed to the *individual now* (1951:300–3; 1962b:42–44, 149–53).

The position of the individual before God is of central importance for Christianity. Thus despite Bultmann's neglect of the social placement of faith and theological reflection, his existential analysis of the individual's move from unfaith to faith continues to be very valuable.

Communal. Bultmann's focus on the individual has been criticized as excessive and as seriously neglectful of the communal and social dimension of human life and history.

Theodor W. Adorno, a representative of the Frankfurt school of critical theory, has given a scathing critique of German existentialist philosophy and of Martin Heidegger in particular—from a Hegelian-Marxist standpoint. Since Bultmann was significantly influenced by Heidegger, Adorno's critique is pertinent. I will give a sketch of Heidegger's analysis of authentic and inauthentic existence, which will display the similarity between Heidegger and

Bultmann and, at the same time, the object of Adorno's unsparing criticism.

Heidegger's term for the entity that each of us is is *Dasein* (being-there) and its essential character is that it inquires into its being (1962:27). In each case *Dasein* is its possibilities. It has the possibility of being authentic (being its own self) or inauthentic (losing itself), and to be itself authentically it must choose or decide for itself (68, 183). The kind of being that *Dasein* has is defined by its understanding of its being (33, 183).

Dasein loses itself, or is not itself, when it is absorbed in the world that is its concern (163, 216). This is to be dispersed into the one-like-the-many or the they-self. The they is nothing definite. It is the leveling down of all possibilities into an averageness in which everyone is the other, and no one is herself or himself. This is a publicness in which *Dasein* has fallen away from the potentiality for being its self (164–68, 220).

The authentic self, on the other hand, has taken hold of its own way (164–68). By anticipating death as its inescapable, ownmost possibility—the possibility that most radically defines a person—*Dasein* is wrenched away from the they. Having found its ownmost self by anticipating death, one is freed from lostness in the accidental—nonessential—possibilities that thrust themselves upon us in the world. One is thereby liberated to understand authentically and to choose among the factical—concrete, historical—possibilities that lie on this side of death. That is, one may choose those concrete possibilities that will actualize one's ownmost, authentic self rather than those that belong to the they-self. This individualizes *Dasein* down to itself (279, 284, 307–9, 395). Anticipating death shatters one's tenacious attachment to whatever existence one has reached and enables *Dasein* to move into the future as a coming-toward-oneself (308, 385).

For Heidegger it is possible for *Dasein* to choose authenticity because in conscience the self calls the self out of the publicness and inauthenticity of the they. Authenticity is thus a modification of the they, and *Dasein* is both the caller and the called. The call gives no information about the world; nothing is called to the self.

Rather the self is summoned to its ownmost potentiality for being (312–20).

Theodor Adorno's *The Jargon of Authenticity* argues that the discourse of existentialism is a jargon in that it breaks language down into words and then seeks to find the meaning of these isolated words, not in historical usage, but in some alleged ancient and magical point of origin. The words are expected to have their impact just from their delivery and without regard for content and are expected to sound as if they mean more than they mean. Some of the key words of the jargon are: authenticity, existential, decision, encounter, and concern (Adorno, 6–9, 42, 49–50, 58).

For Adorno, Heidegger's distinguishing of the authentic self from the public they-self and his insistence on the individual self's owning itself ignore the determining reality of the objective social order in which the individual exists. The individual is thereby deprived of the specific attributes that define him or her, and the self withdraws into its abstract selfhood emptied of all qualities. Adorno questions how something so thinned down can be said to exist authentically (115, 122, 128, 135, 137).

Adorno's criticism of Heidegger is ethical as well as philosophical. Heidegger wants to insert romanticized social constructs from a simple, agrarian past into the present in a way that is thoroughly incompatible with current economic conditions. The existentialist babble prevents truly harmful socioeconomic structures and the disparity between wealth and poverty from being recognized and criticized (Adorno, 47, 59–60, 66, 68–69, 96–100).

Actually the Heidegger of *Being and Time* (1962; first published in German in 1927)—one of the works that most influenced Bultmann and the one that Adorno most frequently refers to—does not interpret authentic existence in quite as abstract a way as Adorno charges. Recall that the authentic self can choose factical—concrete, historical—possibilities that are appropriate to the state of authenticity. But John D. Caputo has pointed out that after the 1920s Heidegger dropped all references to "factical life" and turned more and more to the origin and essential being of poetry, art, thinking, and being itself. The call of being drowned out the call of the concrete other, which is also the call of justice. Heidegger made pronouncements about essential homelessness and destruction as opposed to real, factical homelessness and suffering (1993:73–74). The political and ethical implications of Heidegger's philosophy and the relationship of that philosophy to his espousal of Nazism have been hotly debated since the 1980s, but it is far beyond the purpose of this book to pursue that controversy.

Finally, Adorno made a brief, passing critical reference to Bultmann himself (Adorno, 77). In *Jesus and the Word* (1958a), Bultmann stated that his intention was *not* to give *information* about antiquity but to generate a *dialogue* with history that would yield a highly personal *encounter* with the Jesus of history. He wanted to show how Jesus' purpose confronted us with the question of how we are to interpret our own existence (3–4, 6, 8, 10–11). For Bultmann this encounter is mediated by Jesus' teaching, especially the word of forgiveness. The word of forgiveness becomes the event of forgiveness for the hearer when it constrains him or her to a decision. Thus is opened up a relationship between speaker and hearer. The truth of the word has no (informational) attestation outside of itself but is confirmed only by the reality of the forgiveness that occurs in the relationship mediated by the word (10, 217–19).

According to Adorno this view of encounter and interpersonal relationship as the locale of truth deprives encounter of its literal concreteness, defames the objectivity of truth and promotes irrationalism (16, 77–78, 81).

Bultmann has been criticized pointedly by members of the theological guild in terms very like those that Adorno uses against Heidegger. I mention two examples.

Dorothee Soelle wants to develop her political theology in conversation with Bultmann, for the move from existential to political theology is a consequence of his position (1974:2). Bultmann's view that theological statements are true when they answer a question posed by the concrete situation has as its logical outcome, not kerygmatic neoorthodoxy, but political theology (22). Bultmann, however, did not himself realize the potential of his hermeneutical position.

For Soelle the proper understanding of existence, even that of the individual, is inconceivable apart from the social context, which shapes our decisions according to our class connections. Bultmann is aware that human beings are determined by their past, but he does not unpack the biological, social and psychological aspects of this limit on freedom. And existential theology neglects the impact of its own social location on its hermeneutical pre-understanding (43, 45).

Bultmann is wrong to reduce the meaning of history to the existence of the individual—even if the individual is understood socially—and to posit that meaning as always present. Present history cannot have meaning for those imprisoned in the ghetto (Soelle, 48–49). Nor is it permissible to interpret the Gospel pericopes' call to faith in purely personal terms, for these proclamations were public scandals with political consequences for those concerned (14). If love and justice are interpreted apart from their political implications, they are typically adapted to serve the status quo (34–36).

Soelle maintains that Bultmann lacks reflection on the relationship of faith to politics (55). Her political theology does not want to substitute political science for theology nor let practice swallow up reflection. It is a hermeneutical horizon that understands politics as the decisive scheme in which Christian truth becomes practice (58–59). Political theology does not suppress the question of the meaning of individual existence, but it says that that question can be answered only in terms of social conditions and hope. No one can be saved alone but only as a participant in the political mediation of life to everyone in society (60).

Bultmann wrongly views history as having come to an end and interprets redemption as escape from the world. This position itself, however, has political implications, for it accepts the suffering of the social order (Soelle, 62–63). There should be a place for participatory decision-making with a view to change in social structures and not just in individuals (44).

Gareth Jones's *Bultmann: Towards a Critical Theology* (1991) offers a similar critique of Bultmann. Jones fears that Bultmann is in danger of being forgotten and his significance for contemporary theology lost. He wants to overcome that threat by setting forth a critical theology that would generate renewed interest in Bultmann and illuminate his promise. This can be done only by criticizing the weak points in order to salvage what is still useful (2, 4, 126, 163).

Jones is critical of Bultmann's strong tendency to direct his theological interpretation of the New Testament almost exclusively to the one-to-one relationship between God and the individual believer. True, Jesus did call people to a personal encounter with God, but Bultmann was not justified in rejecting so much else in the tradition (128–29, 155, 167–68, 203). Specifically Bultmann pays too little attention to the semantic or metaphorical representation of the Jesus story because of his conviction that there can be only one way of understanding that representation—the eschatological way (139–40).

Bultmann characterizes freedom in Christ as release from all worldly conditions and radical openness to God, but it is this disengagement from worldly conditions that is the root of his theological inadequacy. His theology floats away from the everyday world of the believer (206–7). Bultmann does not articulate what love entails for the believer's course of action in the world (204). Nor does he take account of the impact of the social, economic, and political context on the believer's response to the gospel or on the pre-understanding of the interpreter of Scripture (71, 168–70, 203).

Bultmann was apparently unable to respond to social and political events. His theology showed a lack of social and political concern, and thus he abandoned the reality of existence in time. At its worst Bultmann's exaltation of the believer's encounter with God and elevation above the world sounds like an accommodation to the anxiety of a consumer society without any contribution to the social or political rebuilding of that society (141, 181, 183–85). If Bultmann's theological interpretation of the New Testament is to make a further contribution, it must be politically anchored in the real world (185, 207).

Jones believes that Bultmann's theology does have elements of continuing validity, but in order to be fruitful they must be synthesized with and reformulated by means of sociopolitical concerns. In Jones's judgment Bultmann's most significant contribution to modern hermeneutics is his introduction of pre-understanding and the hermeneutical circle into post-war theology (136). There is also something to be learned from this understanding of theology as *Glaubenslehre*—the teaching of faith. For Bultmann theology is education in how to make one's way to God and how to be in God's presence (3, 20, 31, 126). Thus it gives guidance about how to encounter the risen Lord. And if we grant that liberation theology or political theology still has a place for the individual to have such an encounter, then Bultmann may make a contribution to the personal element in liberation theology (199).

In Jones's judgment the primary theological issue for Bultmann was the relationship between time and eternity, and he holds Bultmann to have made a unique contribution to this problem. Jones is asking how contemporary theology might restore this crucial theme to the central place that it deserves (150, 163, 207). If that is to happen, Bultmann's insights must be anchored in the real world so that the encounter with God can be grasped in the everyday events of life (207–8).

As Jones interprets Bultmann, eschatology is existence in God's presence and thus a dimension beyond the objective world of space and time. But it is also the decisive moment in human existence (Jones, 40–45). That is, it is the moment in which time and eternity intersect, the moment of the encounter with God through the risen Christ (199, 202). Bultmann's focus on the eschatological event as God's encountering the individual is a lasting contribution (192–93).

However, the emphasis on the individual must give way to an emphasis on the social group, and eschatology must be reconnected to a future that holds out hope for effective change. The Spirit should not be understood solely as an aid to the individual quest for identity but also as the power to teach and effect change (Jones, 186–88).

An upshot of these critiques of Bultmann, with which I concur, is that comprehensive treatments of New Testament theology and

New Testament ethics should not be set forth in separation from each other and that the hermeneutical vantage point for interpreting the New Testament should be sociopolitical as well as philosophical (existentialist). I had these goals in mind in my publications of 1985, 1990, and 1997.

In my judgment Bultmann's inattention to the sociopolitical dimension of human existence is a weakness in his New Testament theology. But his position is perhaps more dialectical—or at times simply contradictory—and the flaw less deep and encompassing than the critics sometimes acknowledge. Bultmann can say, as Jones (206) charges, that freedom in Christ means release from all worldly conditions (Bultmann 1960b:241). Bultmann, however, in light of his interpretation of Paul and John, has a dialectical view of the world. Thus he does not mean that the believer is free from the world in the sense of God's creation but free from bondage to the world as fallen, as identical with the flesh, as a demonic power that entices human beings to seek the source of life in the finite rather than in the transcendent (1951:235, 237, 239, 244, 254, 257–59; 1954:18–20; 1955a:15–17; 1969:166–67). Or Bultmann can say that the concrete situation in which a person becomes a believer does not mean anything and, therefore, there is no need to change the external situation as such. But what that means is that God puts a claim on people in whatever actual concrete situation they live in; thus there is no particular external situation that identifies a person as Christian. None of this is a demand for passive nonaction (1969:74–75).

Bultmann has made it clear that "existence" for him has nothing to do with the "inner man" isolated from historical encounters (1951:182; 1955b:259–60), and he can affirm that interpretation should keep in view the concreteness of such categories as materiality, political situations, gender, and family role, for this is where God encounters us (1960b:159, 163). And yet he can say that for the believer nothing has changed outwardly in the world, but the believer's inward relationship to the world has radically changed (1951:20, 22). If this only means, as above, that no particular cultural situation is the necessary sign for being a Christian, then it is not dangerous. But it is too easily read as saying that no social change is necessary.

There is a basis in principle for a positive social ethic in Bultmann's interpretation of one of his favorite Pauline texts—1 Cor 7:29-31. The believer lives in the world "as though not." Christians may be involved in marriage, friendship, buying and selling, and other structures of the social order because these things belong to the goodness of God's creation. But in faith they are distanced or detached or aloof from this world as a power that tempts them to trust such social constructs as the source of ultimate well-being (Bultmann 1951:351; 1954:20–22).

The believer's detachment from the world is not an ascetic rejection that regards the world's materiality as evil. It is rather freedom that allows believers to live in the world and be involved in it without being under its power. Believers, knowing that their grounding is in God, are delivered from anxiety about whether the structures of the world can provide final security. Thus they are free to enjoy fellowship in community because they need not fear the community nor feel the need to manipulate it (Bultmann 1954:20–22).

It must be said that Bultmann gives much more attention to believers' freedom or detachment from the world than to their detached involvement in the world. The latter, if pursued, could give rise to an existential analysis of the individual as ontologically—in principle—social and to an ethic for sociopolitical change. In the end, Bultmann's suggestive moves toward a sociopolitical hermeneutic do not deeply affect the texture of his New Testament theology.

James M. Robinson

The twofold task of New Testament theology according to Robinson is: (1) to give a historical analysis of the texts of primitive Christianity, and (2) to hear these texts in such a way as to express their valid content so that it can emerge as a serious alternative for modern times (the hermeneutical-normative task) (1976:17).

The present questionability of New Testament theology is not whether the New Testament can be understood historically but whether it can be understood theologically as laying a claim on us today (18).

This crisis was precipitated, in Robinson's judgment, by the fact that William Wrede, around the turn of the twentieth century, brought New Testament theology to its end; and Robinson believes that Wrede's main arguments are still convincing (17). Recall that for Wrede New Testament theology should be a strictly historical study of the early Christian religion.

Of course, scholars across the twentieth century continued to produce New Testament theology, despite Wrede; but these Robinson relegates to the never-never land of the living dead (17). He gives attention, for example, to realized eschatology (Dodd), salvation history (Cullmann), and historical reconstruction of the New Testament's time-conditioned thought-world (Conzelmann). These and other practitioners of these modes of New Testament theology intended to write New Testament *theology*, to make the New Testament pertinent for today, but all they did was to report what people had once thought in a way that made their positions fit only for the antique shop (18–19).

Whether or not all of these types of New Testament theology have failed as badly as Robinson thinks—which I doubt (see my discussion of Dodd in chapter 4)—Robinson has overestimated the magnitude of Wrede's near-fatal blow to New Testament theology. That is, Wrede did not give reasoned arguments that the hermeneutical-normative task *cannot* be done. He rather made prescriptive assertions that it *should not* be attempted, and these assertions are based on his excessive expectations for objective historiography.

Given Robinson's interpretation of the situation, one alternative that he sees for the future of New Testament theology is to concede that Wrede was right and let New Testament theology be reduced to the history of the primitive Christian religion (20).

The second alternative, the one that Robinson affirms, is to develop the new front opened up by Bultmann (17, 18, 20).

Bultmann, as we have seen, devised a method for getting below the conscious thought level of the text to a latent understanding of existence that really belonged to the text but could lay a relevant claim upon us today. He thus brought to expression a whole overlooked dimension of early Christianity (20). Bultmann interpreted this understanding of existence anthropologically—for what it revealed about humankind (20–21).

Our present task is not to perpetuate Bultmann's anthropological terminology and position but to extend the use of his method to open up other dimensions of the New Testament's understanding of existence. This understanding has implications for our grasp of history, ontology (how the *being* of things comes to expression), cosmology (how the world is to be grasped), and politics. This program will require recourse to linguistics and the use of the computer (20–22).

John R. Donahue

Donahue regards Bultmann as clearly the leading New Testament theologian of the twentieth century (1996:251). In a formal way Donahue's own approach parallels Bultmann's concern for both history and hermeneutics but differs from Bultmann in specifics.

If Ranke's "how it really happened" is taken as the touchstone for historical objectivity, then Bultmann's historical method is probably more objective than the "new historicism" that Donahue appeals to as a fruitful perspective for articulating New Testament theology. Bultmann upholds the historical method emanating from the Enlightenment (1955a:251), regards the discovery of the historical context as necessary for interpretation, accepts the closed continuum of cause and effect in the historical process (1960b:291–92), and speaks confidently of tracing the historical developments of traditions from their origins (1963:1–6). This may sound quite different from the ethos of the new historicism, which denies historical determinism, questions the possibility of an objectively verifiable past, and thinks of historical meaning as not discovered by the historian but rather as constructed by him or her as a reflection of his or her own situation (Donahue 1996:268–71).

Bultmann, however, is not as far from the new historicism as may first appear to be the case. He fully acknowledges the operation of the *hermeneutical* circle in *historical* scholarship (1963:5). The historian, as a result of his or her existential encounter with history, chooses, out of his or her subjectivity, the point of view from which the historical phenomenon is to be seen. This point of view may be political, social, economic, existential, etc. From each point of view something objective may be seen, but no point of view can grasp the whole phenomenon or the thing "in itself." Reality is seen but from the slant of a limited point of view (1962b:115–22). This subjective element is not a defect. In fact, the most objective interpretation comes from the one who is most deeply engaged in the material from the subjectively chosen point of view (1955b:256).

We see then that for Bultmann, as for the new historicism, historical study is a hermeneutical move. Bultmann is far from the empiricism of, say Ranke, Wrede, and Stendahl, who intend to compartmentalize history and hermeneutics. Perhaps we could say that at the level of philosophy of history—reflection on the relationship between historical phenomena and discourse about them—Bultmann and the new historicism are not far apart; but at the level of doing or writing actual historical scholarship (see White 1989a:21) the new historicism would claim less objectivity then Bultmann does.

With regard to the spectrum of hermeneutical methods or approaches, Donahue represents a definite move beyond Bultmann. Bultmann had in mind essentially two options—historical and existential. Donahue has in view a much fuller repertoire of possibilities. In addition to the new historicism, he sees the relevance of several types of contemporary literary criticism, the related rhetorical criticism, and social-scientific interpretation (1996:255–66, 273).

On the matter of the theological point of view that is to guide biblical interpretation Donahue is discernibly different from Bultmann in terminology if not in concept. Donahue does not speak of the New Testament's offering a new understanding of existence as Bultmann does but declares that the description of religious experience is at the basis of theological construction. Donahue has been influenced by Edward Schillebeeckx's stress on experience as contrasted with Bultmann's theology of the word. According to Schillebeeckx, Christianity is not a message that must be believed but an experience of faith that becomes a message, a message that hopes to offer a new possibility of experience to others. Influenced also by David Tracy, Donahue states that the proper subject matter of New Testament theology is the power of the New Testament texts, which reflect the religious experience of the early Christians (Donahue 1989:325, 335; 1996:274).

Social-scientific methods of critical interpretation are important because by illuminating the social context of early Christianity they give concrete shape to how Christian communities experienced salvation. At the same time literary criticism is important to New Testament theology because the language that brings the religious experience to expression is of theological significance (1989:327–28, 334).

Finally, in employing the terminology of Stephen Greenblatt, the principal originator of the new historicism, Donahue suggests that the challenge of New Testament theology is to enable the power represented in the New Testament texts to resonate in the reader/beholder in such a way as to evoke a sense of wonder, to evoke an exalted attention (1996:273–75). But then Bultmann can say, following R. G. Collingwood, that genuine historical knowledge occurs when imagination allows the events from the past to "vibrate in the historian's mind" (1962b:122, 132–33).

Robin Scroggs

For Scroggs, New Testament theology entails two things: (1) a coherent, structured description of the faith claims of the New Testament texts; (2) the use of such descriptions to inform the faith affirmations of subsequent generations of believers (1988:17). The increasing sophistication of recent social-scientific and historical criticism poses a threat to both of these aspects. The social and political situations of the various New Testament texts have been shown to be so discretely particular and the messages of these texts so tied to these particularities that it becomes questionable whether we can identify coherent theological connections among these texts. By the same token the New Testament period and our time are so distant from each other in their particularity that it becomes questionable whether we can discover an analogy between the New Testament and our situation(s) that would allow the former to aid our contemporary theological thinking (18–19, 22).

A further problem has arisen from the demonstration that Paul's letters were shaped by Greco-Roman rhetoric—the "art of persuasion." Some conclude from this that we, therefore, cannot know what Paul thought but only what he wanted his readers to think that he taught (20).

Scroggs has some suggestions about how we might save New Testament theology in both its aspects and in such a way that scholarly research would not be constrained but the New Testament would still be empowered to lay a claim upon us in our present situation (23, 26). Scroggs finds a fruitful basis for his proposals in Hans-Georg Gadamer's understanding of interpretation as a conversation between text and interpreter in which each speaks from its own horizon with a view to the fusion of the horizons. This approach would enable us to acknowledge the truth claims of the text without imposing dogmatics on it (24–25).

Regarding the question of whether we can really know what Paul thought, Scroggs's proposal is that interpretation should not try to deal with the self-consciousness or subjective intention of the author but with the intention of the text. If what the text says is true, it is true irrespective of the factors that led to the production of the text (26–28).

With regard to the threat to coherence engendered by the multiplicity of highly particular contexts Scroggs's recommendation is that interpretation should bring to light the tensions among the texts while holding out the expectation that these tensions are restrained by an overarching coherency. This expectation may or may not be in fact fulfilled. In finding a possible coherency among the texts the interpreter's horizon also comes into the picture, and that creates a coherency between the New Testament and the interpreter's present situation (29–30).

It is appropriate to point out here that Wolfgang Iser has developed a theory of reading that sees the task of the critical reader as achieving congruences that did not exist in the text (1980:9–10, 14–15, 17, 19–25, 27, 30, 38, 92, 135, 141, 150, 152).

Robert W. Funk

Funk's *Honest to Jesus* (1996) takes a definite position on the relationship between history and hermeneutics and is informative because it expresses one—though not the only—outlook held in the Jesus Seminar. It is not inappropriate to discuss Funk's book in our exploration of the task of New Testament theology because in a strong sense the historical Jesus is the sole object of Funk's theological and hermeneutical concerns. In Funk's opinion most of the reflections about Jesus from Nicea forward and from Nicea backward, including the Gospels, Paul, and even the oral traditions, are distortions that should be rejected (45, 135, 241, 250–52).

Funk maintains programmatically that critical history and religion should be kept in dialectical interaction. What we believe religiously should be informed by facts so far as we can discover them (2–3). The historical goal of the quest for the historical Jesus is factual information, what can be observed, and without regard for religious interests (2–3, 21–25, 26, 29).

Funk seems to separate the historical-critical and the hermeneutical moments in interpretation, but once he has established what he regards as the historically reliable elements in the Jesus tradition by the use of critical principles, he is quite interested in the hermeneutical potential of that material. The theological purpose of the quest for the historical Jesus, negatively speaking, is to allow the historical Jesus to subvert later interpretations of Jesus, both popular and scholarly, to overthrow orthodox Christology (19–20). The positive theological goal is to set Jesus free from prevailing captivities. Jesus could thus emerge as a larger-than-life figure in his own right (21, 60, 300). Jesus, rather than the Bible or the creeds, should become the norm for a reformed Christianity (300–1, 306).

Specifically, for example, Funk suggests that Jesus be demoted from the status of divine Son co-eternal with the Father so that he might be more available to us (306). Jesus should be given a role in a new myth. Take him out of the story of the external redeemer (akin to Superman) who descends from another world, spends a brief time here, and then returns to the alien world. See him rather as a hero who begins in the real world, leaves home for an alien space, undergoes trials and achieves victory over evil, returns home, and is reintegrated into society with power to help (the myth underlying the Synoptic temptation stories) (306–10).

One interesting deconstructive slippage in Funk's project is worth noting. It perhaps reveals the difficulty/impossibility of trying to separate sharply the historical and hermeneutical moments. Funk observes that the historical Jesus associates with social outcasts, engages in celebratory meals, and tells parabolic stories about the celebrations. Thus, says Funk, Jesus acts in accordance with a transfixing vision that both captivated and liberated him. The parables do not refer to Jesus, but he is on the edge as a listener, ready to risk the consequences of his own vision (161–62, 189, 248).

The affirmations in the previous paragraph make assumptions about Jesus' subjectivity, inner dispositions, or existential wholeness. These assertions are not subject to historical validation. They do not belong to the realm of what can be observed. Rather they are christological claims—and may be quite correct—but are not historically verifiable. They grow out of faith and are examples of faith seeking understanding. They are attempts to make conceptual (theological) sense of faith's encounter with Jesus.

N. T. Wright

Because Wright's project is very large in scope and because he is a much-read contemporary scholar, his position deserves considerable attention.

The Hermeneutical Circle

For Wright New Testament theology is clearly both historical and hermeneutical, theologically relevant today (1992:16, 18–20, 24–25). But his program is too complex and expansive to be confined to these two categories. In Wright's approach, a theological understanding of the New Testament requires both historical and literary interpretation (25–27, 139), and all of these categories are comprehended within a hermeneutical process that he calls critical realism. This is his basic position about how people know anything. Critical realism acknowledges that we can know reality outside of ourselves, but this knowledge about the other is always grasped by means of—seen through the lens of—our own story or worldview. Thus knowledge is always marked by the knower's subjective vantage point and is therefore provisional. Acquiring knowledge is a continuing dialogue between knower and the known (32, 35–37, 43, 64, 124–25).

This view of the hermeneutical circle (14, 121, 138) and of how knowledge is acquired (19) deeply affects Wright's position on how understanding is gained by historical and literary criticism. Regarding history, we will never know "how it really happened"— though we can certainly know something—because history writing always involves selection made from an interpretative point of view that wants to make sense of events (1992:15, 82–83, 85–89). The goal of historical inquiry is to understand human beings from the inside (91). Regarding literature, we understand the stories that we read in light of the stories that already shape our existence, while being open to the possibility that the other stories, including those in the New Testament, may affirm, modify, or subvert our own private stories (66–67).

Worldviews

The concept of worldview is central for Wright's program. A society's or person's worldview is the presuppositional, precognitive sense of what is of ultimate importance, the lens through which everything else is seen. Worldviews provide the stories through which human beings view reality; in fact stories are the best clues about the import of a worldview (1992:40, 122–24, 140). From these stories people can discover how to answer the questions that define human existence: who are we, where are we, what is wrong, what is the solution (123).

Worldviews become articulate in sets of basic beliefs and aims that in turn generate consequent beliefs and aims (125–26).

Historical Criticism

For Wright historical criticism is methodologically necessary for New Testament theology in order to avoid over-assimilating the past to the present, to preserve the particularity of the past, to prevent remaking Jesus in our own image (1992:9–10; 1996:52–53). And it is theologically necessary because of the biblical view that God is involved in the historical process. What happened in history matters theologically (1992:9–10; 1996:9, 122, 137, 661).

Methodologically, Wright rejects the form critical approach (still used putatively by the Jesus Seminar) that evaluates isolated bits of evidence by the use of criteria of various sorts. Instead he seeks to establish a comprehensive hypothesis or big picture that tests, and is tested by, small-scale decisions about evidence (1992:98–100, 103, 108–9; 1996:33, 79, 87–88).

At the end of his full discussion of hermeneutical method, Wright stresses the vital importance of setting out the historical context of the New Testament (1992:144). This is a revealing declaration, for he does in fact describe at length the Jewish context in which Jesus lived and the church emerged. But his historical reasoning about the historicity of certain phenomena narrated or referred to in the New Testament raises puzzling questions.

Some will think that Wright's big picture of a highly messianic historical Jesus (1996:128, 529–39, 648–49) who intended, predicted, and theologically interpreted his death (466, 540–611) has overwhelmed appropriate critical decisions about individual elements. Wright criticizes others for failing to think historically (1996:470), but scholars differ about when such failures occur. I will give some examples of this problem.

In discussing the historicity of the Last Supper, Wright argues that Jesus himself did celebrate the meal with his disciples as some kind of Passover. To question this is to engage in "radical skepticism" (1996:554–56). Similarly, he states that it is "incredible" that the early church should have inserted Jesus' actions with the bread and cup apart from a firm basis in Jesus' own actions (558). To argue for a particular historical construction on the ground that an alternative view is radically skeptical or incredible seems questionable.

With regard to the confession of Peter that Jesus is the Messiah, Wright seems to hold that the confession itself, Jesus' tacit acceptance of the title, the command of secrecy, the suffering Son of Man motif, the call to allegiance, and the prediction of the coming kingdom constitute a credible sequence (Mark 8:27—9:1) in light of the Jewish context of messianic claimants (1996:470–72, 528–30). The first thing to be said is that credibility or plausibility is an argument for possibility but is not a strong argument for probability. Historical fiction may be quite plausible and often is. And Mark—however much historical material it may contain—is a fiction. It is shaped by plot, characterization, irony, metaphor, etc. But these are nonspecific reasons for questioning the historicity of the sequence in Mark 8:27—9:1.

Mark 8:27—9:1 is composed of *different kinds* of traditional material; therefore, it could hardly have emanated from the same source. Someone has put together items from disparate sources or collections. Since 8:27—9:1 is an integral part of an obviously Markan composition composed of 8:27—10:52, it is probable that the smaller unit, 8:27—9:1 is also a Markan composition.

This present discussion is an obvious example of how literary criticism should affect historical judgments. Mark 8:27—10:52 is a section highly poeticized by an elaborate employment of parallelism and threefoldness. There are three predictions of what will happen to the Son of Man (8:31; 9:31; 10:33-34). Each of these predictions has three parts—suffering, death and resurrection. Each of these predictions is a part of a threefold structure composed of prediction, some indication of misunderstanding on the part of the disciples and a teaching by Jesus on the nature of discipleship (8:31—9:1; 9:31-37; 10:32-52).

Parallelism causes the parallel or similar linguistic elements to refer to each other. Thus, the language of Mark 8:27—10:52 is characterized by a tight network of internal self-reference. This is the poetic function of language, and this *internal self-reference* of language diminishes, but does not destroy, the capacity of that stretch of language to refer outside of itself to nonlinguistic phenomena (Jacobson 1972:90, 93, 95–96, 112). Therefore, one cannot lift individual items out of such a poetic configuration and regard them as historical without more argumentation than Wright has given.

Wright claims to be a historian in dealing with the question of the virginal conception of Jesus by means of the Holy Spirit (1999a:172). What is troubling about his procedure is that he argues *from* his *belief* that God was fully revealed in Jesus and raised him bodily from the dead *to* the possible or probable *fact* of the virginal conception (172, 176, 178). Wright might defend this move by arguing that all history involves imaginative reconstruction. There is always a leap to be made between the actual evidence and a full-blown reconstruction (1996:8). Wright is right about this. But in historical work, the imaginative leap is *from fragmentary historical evidence to a coherent historical narrative*. It is *not from religious or theological beliefs to historical reconstruction*. Wright himself argues that the rigorous history that he intends to pursue is an open-ended investigation of actual events in first-century Palestine, an investigation whose results are not determined in advance (1996:8). But if a religious belief (God was fully present in Jesus and raised him from the dead) that one *already* holds when he or she takes up a historical question is allowed to influence strongly the outcome (Jesus was probably conceived in a virgin), then the investigation was not open-ended.

At the level of theological reflection Wright's holding to the probability of the virginal conception of Jesus does not take account of Bultmann's primary objection to myth—that it undermines the transcendence of God. That is, if the Holy Spirit literally generated a child in the womb of Mary, it is impossible to escape the conclusion that God's creative power is assimilated to, in fact, is identified with, the male procreative function. Transcendence is thereby compromised. Wright seems to lack a sense of the theological import of Bultmann's definition of myth and of the need to demythologize (1992:425).

Literary Criticism

For Wright literature is neither a neutral description of the world nor a collection of subjective feelings. Human writing is best conceived as the telling of stories that bring worldviews into articulation (1992:65).

Wright raises the question of what kind of knowledge we gain when we read stories and recognizes that the answer is complex to the point of being confusing (1992:50, 53). He acknowledges that a reading always expresses subjectively the reader's particular situation and that readers encounter in the text meanings and structures that exceed the author's intention. Nevertheless, Wright also insists that reading should take account of the integrity and impact of the text itself, the author's intention, and the author's references to events outside of his or her own mind (1992:61–64).

When reading becomes critical a significant part of its task is to lay bare a work's implied worldview and show how it came to expression. The latter will entail giving attention to such elements as plot, character, rhetorical techniques, irony, conflict, etc. Wright's method of narrative analysis is to employ some of the structuralist categories of A. J. Greimas, not in a narrowly formalist way, but as assimilated to Wright's hermeneutical concerns. Wright, for example, employs some of Greimas's constructions to show how in Luke and Matthew the interactions among characters advance the plot (1992:39, 65, 70–80, 382–84, 389–90). For Wright if biblical theological interpretation is working properly, the interpreter—through the lens of his or her own stories—will grasp the whole of the Bible as a complex five-act comedy (1992:66–67, 140–42).

In Wright's long discussion of the "Stories of the Kingdom," the short narratives by and about Jesus in the Synoptic Gospels, he tends to present these narratives as allegories that both retell and subvert the story of Israel, with Jesus as the culminating climax of that story. If one assumes the reader-response theory of literary interpretation and thereby holds that readers as well as authors contribute to the meaning of texts, then Wright's interpretation is one possibility. The three chapters on the short narratives are an elaborate tissue of Wright's allegorical *reading* of the stories. But when Wright maintains, as he regularly does, that this reading represents the intention of Jesus or the original meaning of the stories, he is unconvincing.

At this point a comparison between Bultmann and Wright might be instructive. For Bultmann the category for connecting the New Testament to the contemporary situation is an understanding of existence, while for Wright the category is story. This is a clear difference in emphasis and in part a difference in principle, but they are not as unlike as they may appear to be. Both make use of the concept of worldview. For Wright story is the best key to the meaning of a worldview, and for Bultmann an understanding of existence entails a worldview, a depiction of the transcendent power that controls the world and humankind (1954:3, 10–11; 1960a:3). Moreover, Wright is concerned about existential questions (1992:91, 109, 123), and Bultmann is prepared to accept the use of story and other kinds of symbolic language in religious and theological discourse. But on this last point the two are significantly different.

For Wright, story is crucial. Bultmann, on the other hand, allows that symbol and image are *perhaps* (my italics) necessary to the language of religion, but then he seems to say that language about God's acting does *not necessarily* (my italics) require symbol and image, though it may require us to use analogues to human action that can be conceptually articulated (1958b:67–69). In the final analysis Bultmann apparently regarded symbolic language as inherently dangerous. It always threatens to mislead the interpreter into taking it literally, thereby regarding God as an object (1960a:3). On the issue of the use and importance of imagistic language Wright is ahead of Bultmann.

In two related ways Wright—not to mention Scroggs and Donahue—has made a positive move beyond Bultmann. (1) He grasps the cruciality of story and other figurative forms for the language of faith. (2) He sees the importance of a literary criticism that takes the New Testament seriously as literature. The literary qualities of a story—plot, metaphor, etc.—have an important bearing on the theological meaning.

Theology

Theology can be defined in a narrowly focused way as the study of the gods or God. But Wright tends to a more inclusive definition. Worldviews provide stories, and stories suggest varying answers to the basic questions of existence. These stories, questions, and answers are the subject matter of theology. A good deal of Christian theology consists of trying to tell the biblical story as clearly as possible and of allowing it to subvert other ways of telling the world's story. Theology also debates issues pertaining to the basic and consequent beliefs that grow out of worldviews (1992:123, 125–26, 129, 132, 134).

Very summarily, the Bible answers the basic questions of existence as follows. Who are we: human beings created in the image of God. Where are we: in a good and beautiful though transient world created by God. What is wrong: humanity rebelled against the creator and caused a severe disruption. What is the solution: the creator has acted, is acting, and will act—primarily in Jesus and the Spirit—to deal with the evil caused by the human rebellion (1992:132–33).

But Wright also wants to deal specifically with the question of God, which, he correctly notes, is usually neglected in books about the New Testament. The God question, he observes, is generally at the root of the various issues that the New Testament writers raise. And these writers are not assuming but are rather inquiring into what the term *God* (which Wright generally spells with a small g) means (1992:471). Early Christianity was monotheistic as Judaism was and paganism was not. But Christian monotheism necessarily entailed claims about Christ, the Spirit, and the church. And in the final analysis the New Testament's assertions about Jesus distinguished Christianity in principle from both Judaism and paganism (457–58, 475–76).

Existential Interpretation and Demythologizing

I have observed that in certain ways Wright moves beyond Bultmann. But Wright makes other claims to have surpassed Bultmann that are not convincing and that involve, in my opinion, misrepresentations of Bultmann's position. One instance of the latter is Wright's contention that when Bultmann does theology by doing anthropology he follows Ludwig Feuerbach in collapsing God-talk into man-talk (1957:89–90). But Wright has turned a superficial similarity between Feuerbach and Bultmann into a material identity.

It is true that both scholars say aphoristically that "theology is anthropology" (Feuerbach 1957:xxxvii; Bultmann 1951:191). But the entailments of this statement are very different for the two scholars. For Feuerbach it means that there is no distinction between the divine and human predicates and hence none between the divine and human subjects. God is the manifested, expressed, projected inward self of the person, purified and objectified and contemplated as if it were other than human. Religion fails to grasp the identity of the divine and human and treats the divine as if it were other (xxxvii, 12–14, 29–30, 33, 185, 284).

For Bultmann's theology there is a real distinction between God and humankind. In fact, the justification for Bultmann's claim that God and human existence must be spoken of together is Bultmann's belief that God is the Almighty who determines all else (1969:53, 55).

The only theological statements that are legitimate are those that express the engaged existential situation of the speaker. General, universal statements about God that do not manifest God's connection to specific existential issues are attempts to escape my relation to God's all-determining reality. Only engaged statements acknowledge God's sovereignty (1969:53–56). It is only one's concrete existence that can grasp the reality of God (1969:57); thus every assertion about God must simultaneously be an assertion about human existence and vice versa (1951:191). I can affirm that God is the creator of the world only by confessing that I am a creature who owes his existence to God (1958b:69).

The transcendence of God for Bultmann is not just a matter of theological correctness but of existential exigency. Only the one who knows the transcendent God whose word is spoken in Christ can extricate himself or herself from this sinful world (1960b:163).

According to Wright, Bultmann's demythologizing program is a move away from the culture-specific speech forms of the first century to timeless truths (1992:20–21). To this contention it must be rejoined that Bultmann explicitly disclaims the view that his interpretation is definitive for all times (1960a:4). The theological thoughts of the New Testament are not to be treated as timeless, general truths but as an understanding of human existence possible for today. Since interpretation is always determined by the interpreter's situation, all interpretations are incomplete and must be redone by each generation (1955a:237–38, 251).

Nor does Bultmann abandon specificity. His interpretation is aimed at a particular cultural ethos that can no longer accept the prescientific worldview (1954:3–4). Moreover, Bultmann maintains that interpretation should keep in view the concreteness of such categories as nationality, political situation, gender, and family role, for this is where God encounters us (1960b:159, 163).

With reference to the political, for example, Bultmann argues that the antitheses of the Sermon on the Mount—"You have heard . . . but I say to you" (Matt 5:21-48)—show that the state's ordinances of justice fall far short of the demand of God, for the former make no claim on a person's inner disposition. But Jesus does not thereby reject the validity of the state's demand for justice.

The latter is legitimate, if provisional, because the full reign of God is still future. So what God demands is that the individual renounce his or her right to use the ordinances of justice to further her or his own interests against the neighbor. But the antitheses imply that the state's justice is legitimate when it stands in service of love or serves the community (1960b:204–5). But we should recall that Bultmann's tentative moves toward a sociopolitical hermeneutic do not bear substantial fruit.

For Bultmann the word of God comes to us from beyond the world and challenges everything in us and in the world. But its connection to our concrete lives is not lost, for we hear the word of God aright only when we hear it ever anew and in relation to our life decisions. Bultmann seems to envision a dialectic between the voice of God and the voices of the world that come to us out of our duties and destinies, out of nature and history. But he gives priority to the word of God (1960b:167, 169–70).

Thus it cannot be said that Bultmann without qualification abandons the concrete and specific in favor of timeless truths. What his existential interpretation and demythologizing do is to identify an analogy between the particularity of the New Testament text and the particularity of the present-day interpreter: an understanding of existence. This analogy is a point of contact between the two, a point that is to some degree generalizable; otherwise the two particularities could not be connected. One cannot directly translate one particularity into another. It is necessary to grasp a horizon that comprehends both particularities. Bultmann's approach enables the New Testament message to be timely in a multiplicity of particular times, but makes no claim to be timeless.

The difference between Bultmann's and Wright's hermeneutics of New Testament theology becomes especially clear in connection with the issue of eschatology. Wright is critical of Bultmann's demythologizing interpretation of eschatology and believes that his own approach is a way forward beyond Bultmann (1992:20–27, 285–86). Krister Stendahl back in 1962 had reckoned that, whatever one may think about how Bultmann carried out demythologizing, demythologizing was here to stay (1962:422a). Wright's project shows how overly optimistic Stendahl's prediction was.

According to Bultmann early Christianity believed in the near end of the world, a cosmic dissolution, the termination of the time-space order. Because this expectation is mythological in principle and because it did not happen as expected, it is a belief that we should not hold to, but it can be reinterpreted existentially (1954:5; 1960b:249; 1951:4; 1962b:37–38).

Wright strongly disagrees with Bultmann's position. According to Wright, neither Judaism nor early Christianity believed in the end of the world at all. Rather the cosmic language about the new age is metaphor that expresses the immense significance of coming historical events. The kingdom of God to come will be a physical renewal of this world. And the resurrection of the dead will involve the renewal of physical bodies to live in a renewed physical world (1992:284–86, 370, 459–62). It is a this-worldly hope. Wright claims Paul as support for this view, but in his discussion of the early Christian hope in *The New Testament and the People of God* (1992:460–61) he fails to mention that Paul denies that flesh and blood can inherit the kingdom of God but rather attributes a *spiritual* body to the resurrection existence (1 Cor 15:44, 50).

In a more recent article, however, Wright does treat 1 Corinthians 15:42-56 and tries to maintain his position by what, in my opinion, is strained exegesis. He acknowledges Paul's denial that the resurrection body is constituted by flesh and blood, but he then argues that Paul's "spiritual body" does not mean a nonphysical body. It rather has in view a body whose physicality is different from fleshly physicality. It is a new and transformed kind of physicality (1999b:120–27).

But, we must ask, what kind of human physicality has no part in flesh and blood? Wright obviously wants his present-day reader to find that his argument makes sense, but what kind of sense can it make? The ordinary dictionary definition of *physical* focuses on such connotations as material, earthly, tangible, and visible. Thus when Wright expresses the idea of a non-fleshly physical body, he is, in our terms, talking about a nonmaterial material body. What can be made of that?

What prompts Wright to interpret New Testament eschatology as the strictly this-worldly hope for a renewed physical body in a renewed physical creation? He seems to offer the hint of at least a partial explanation. For Wright, the New Testament is both relevant (1992:16, 18–19, 24–25) and authoritative (20, 23, 132, 139–43, 470–72) for today, and he seems to fear that if the New Testament actually expected the near end of the space-time universe and was wrong, that authority would be compromised. That is, if the early Christians really held this central belief in the near end of the world and were mistaken, they would seem so distant from us that we could not take them seriously (1992:285). The only other alternative, if the end-of-the-world interpretation is right, is to try to construct, as Bultmann does, a hermeneutic that will somehow enable us to salvage something from this wreckage (285).

Wright does not think that Bultmann has salvaged anything worthwhile, and he is not prepared to endanger the authority of the New Testament by attributing to it an idea so foreign to our time as the termination of the time-space universe. Thus are generated Wright's claims that the New Testament expects, not the end of the world, but a transformed physical body in a transformed physical world. The anomaly in this move is that it actually threatens the authority of the New Testament in that it is more difficult for us to assimilate his interpretation than to assimilate the cosmic end, especially if the latter is existentially reinterpreted.

There are three levels of problems in Wright's putting forth his position as the normative Christian view. His interpretation of 1 Corinthians 15, which really focalizes the difficulty, implies a proposition something like: the physical (material) resurrection body is non-fleshly (nonmaterial). There is a disjunction between subject and predicate (material is nonmaterial) at the immanent propositional level (see Ricoeur 1976:10, 20).

Second, there is also a problem at the referential level. It is impossible for him to remove the connotation of materiality from the category of the physical, unless Wright is using "physical" in a mysterious sense known only to him. What then can transformed, materially physical bodies in a transformed, materially physical creation refer to? How many billions of people have already lived on this earth and will live on it into the indeterminate future? The prospect of these multiple billions living in even transformed physical bodies in a transformed physical world is not a story that we can tell ourselves at the turn of the millennium.

In the third place, Wright's position is mythological in the precisely Bultmannian sense of myth. It identifies the transcendent—God's eschatological kingdom—with the finite—a *renewed* time-space universe, which is, nevertheless, *still* the *time-space* universe. Even if it turned out that Wright's interpretation was possible at the level of the New Testament's first-century meaning, this would still have to be demythologized if the transcendence of God is to be preserved.

Wright's interpretation of New Testament eschatology does not fit well with his own programmatic hermeneutical position. He understands legitimate interpretation as an interaction between the worldview of the text and the worldview of the interpreter. The resultant meaning will express both a continuity and a discontinuity between these two poles (1992:65–67, 121–22, 138). But in his actual interpretation of eschatology the discontinuity virtually disappears. He assumes that what he takes as the biblical view is to continue unchanged into the theology of the present day Christian. There is no assimilation or naturalization of the biblical story to the contemporary one.

Wright's position turns out to be not so much a move beyond Bultmann as a reversion to a pre-Bultmannian approach. It seems both more realistic and more meaningful to recognize that the New Testament does expect the near end of the world, that this does in fact distance us from the earliest Christians, but that the literal near end can be rejected without losing the crisis note present in biblical eschatology.

For Bultmann, the New Testament—with notable exceptions—expects the kingdom of God as a cosmic catastrophe, the near end of the world. At the same time, this expected future determines the present, for it places humankind under the inescapable necessity of a final decision. Thus the eschatologically determined present can itself be grasped as the dawning or even coming of the kingdom of God (1958a:51–52, 55–56; 1951:4–7; 1962b:37–48). Again, for Bultmann the end of the world is a myth that cannot be literally accepted. But this future, along with the present that it determines, gives outward expression to an understanding of existence that can stand on its own feet independently of its mythological expression. In fact it is the understanding of existence that is the more basic element, for it makes use of the myth to bring itself to expression (1958a:52, 55–56; 1960b:252).

The gospel places human beings between the eschatological event that has already come but is yet to come and thereby gives expression to the paradox of the human situation. The person so placed experiences God as both judge and gracious father. She has been taken out of the past and put in the future but does not yet fully belong to the future. He is a new creation freed from the past but does not have that freedom as a possession. It must be ever laid hold of anew. The believers must become what they already are, and they are already what they shall become (1960b:252–55; 1962b:48).

Finally, it is possible to draw from Paul's image of the spiritual body in 1 Corinthians 15 an understanding of life after death that is different from both the Jewish renewal of the physical body and the Greek immortality of the soul. Whatever the expression "spiritual body" may connote in its fullness, it means at least that the resurrection existence will not be physical (1 Cor 15:50). That the continuing life with God will be spiritual means that the constitutive factor in the spiritual body will be the self as subject, knowing itself and reality outside of itself and open to God (Rom 8:16; 1 Cor 2:10-11; 16:18; 2 Cor 2:13; 7:13; see Via 1990:70–73). That the continuing life with God will be bodily means that the person will have a specific and concrete identity relatable to God and other reality (Via 1990:68–70), but on the other side of death the body will not be physical.

The nonphysicality of the resurrection body does not mean, however, that that body will not be deeply affected by the earlier physical existence on earth. As is well known, in biblical anthropology the human self is a whole or totality and not an aggregation of parts. Therefore, terms like *body, flesh, soul, spirit, heart,* and so forth are not parts of the self but aspects of the whole. This implies that these aspects interpenetrate each other. That being the case, the spiritual body will be indelibly marked by one's former physical, bodily existence.

Having been in the physical body, or rather having *been* a physical body, is constitutive in part of what one will be eternally. The spiritual body will be both continuous and discontinuous with what we have been. It will have a specific identity marked by the physical bodily existence, and it will be open to God without impediment.

Thus we see that a demythologizing, existential hermeneutic can retain significant aspects of Paul's position without falling into the problems created by Wright's approach. In sum, Wright's narrative-theological interpretations of Luke, Matthew, John, and Paul are often illuminating and convincing. Much less satisfactory are his treatment of Mark; his way of employing historical criticism, and the resultant analysis of the historical Jesus; and his method and results in dealing with the problem areas of the New Testament—what Bultmann called myth.

6

New Testament Theology as Hermeneutical: Postmodernism

Modernism and Postmodernism

In order to understand and assess the fact that a number of biblical theologians have bought heavily into postmodernism, we need to take account of the (alleged) shift from modernism to postmodernism. Modernism may be thought to have begun at some time during the Renaissance and then to have become the dominant way of thinking in Europe in the seventeenth century (Reiss 1982:13, 21, 31).

Modernism has been characterized by a rejection of tradition and the authority of the past, a rejection of permanence and transcendent ideals, in favor of novelty, change, and progress (Calinescu 1987:3, 23, 27, 95). The dominating thrust of modernism was to employ reason in order to gain a truly objective knowledge of the real order of the things of the world (Calinescu 1987:27; Reiss 1982:22–23). The purpose of this objective explanation of the world is to enable us to conquer, dominate, and possess it (Reiss 1982:21). The means for achieving this knowledge according to Timothy J. Reiss is a kind of analysis that assumes a fixed, knowable external world that is prior to and separate from the discourse with which we describe it. But language, rational thought, and the order of the world are intervolved with one another. A properly syntactical sentence provides the appropriate rational concepts to refer adequately to the true objective nature of the world (Reiss 1982:21, 23, 29–31, 37, 41). According to Reiss, from the beginning of modernism to the present, this understanding of reality has been the single dominant structure and necessary form to be taken by thought, knowledge, and cultural and social practices of all kinds (23).

In the judgment of Matei Calinescu, a split occurred at some time during the first half of the nineteenth century that produced two forms of modernism (1987:41). (1) Bourgeois, capitalistic modernism sees time as a commodity to be bought and sold. Its ideals are rationality, utility and progress. It is a product of scientific and technological advances, the industrial revolution, and capitalism (5, 10, 41, 45). (2) Aesthetic or cultural modernism understands time as the subjective unfolding of the self. It expressed a hatred for bourgeois commercialism and utilitarianism. It promoted art for art's sake and sought the immediacy of an identification with the present in its very transitoriness. Its sense of being radically new and different from everything that preceded it took on the color of an apocalyptic crisis (Calinescu 1987:5, 10, 41, 45, 47–48, 91; Kermode 1971:40, 46).

Calinescu's analysis may require some modification of Reiss's position that objective rational discourse dominated everything in modernism, and Reiss himself hints at a qualification of his position. In the view of Calinescu the central, underlying motif of all forms of modernism is a concern about the problem of time. The idea of modernity can be conceived within a view of history that sees time as linear, irreversible, unrepeatable, and flowing irresistibly onward. Thus modernism has a real affinity with the Judeo-Christian eschatological view of history (Calinescu 1987:9, 13). Calinescu's point puts into question the contention of postmodern New Testament theologians that the *modernity* of New Testament theology is strictly incompatible with the real concerns of the New Testament.

We may place the beginning of postmodernism in the 1960s, though some would put it a good deal earlier. A variety of causal factors have been urged to account for its emergence (Calinescu 1987:5–6, 275–78; Reiss 1982:11, 21, 37, 259–60), and I will mention two (apparently) quite diverse opinions. According to Terry Eagleton, postmodernism arose, in part, out of the failure of modernity to achieve social justice, out of the political defeat of the left, out of the seeming impossibility or infeasibility of any far-reaching, transforming political action (1997:viii, ix, 1, 9, 10, 20–21). Stanley Hauerwas argues, on the other hand, that postmodernism arose from a fundamental mistake made by Christian theology, the mistake of trying to make God known through nature, separable from God's revelation in Scripture (1999:110–11).

The terms *postmodernism* and *postmodernity* are sometimes distinguished and sometimes used interchangeably. Postmodernity may refer to a style of thought that is suspicious of classical notions of truth, reason, and objectivity. It prefers knowledge that can be translated into quantitative information and computer language to grand narratives that claim to give total explanations. Against Enlightenment norms it sees the world as contingent, ungrounded, diverse, unstable, and indeterminate. Postmodernism may refer to a style of culture that is depthless and playful and that blurs distinctions (Eagleton 1997:vii; Lyotard 1984:xxiii–xxiv, 3–4, 82). Eagleton believes that postmodernism in fact exists and that we are living in it. But it contains inner contradictions, and he wonders how far down it goes and whether it is wall-to-wall (1997:ix, 20, 22).

Ihab Hassan acknowledges the extreme difficulty of clarifying the identity of postmodernism and distinguishing it from modernism (1987:xv, 29, 53, 84–85, 87–88, 167–68). But he does give an interesting list of conflicting characteristics in which the first term represents modernism and the second one, postmodernism: form/antiform, purpose/play, presence/absence, depth/surface, determinacy/indeterminacy, transcendence/immanence (91). Eagleton is critical of postmodernism for working rigidly with binary oppositions and affirming only one side of the oppositions rather than dialectically thinking both sides of them (1997:25–26).

Fredric Jameson can say that one of the comprehensive defining features of postmodernism is the effacement of the frontier between high culture and so-called mass or commercial culture (1984b:54). Or he can suggest that the supreme formal feature of all postmodernism is a new kind of depthlessness, a new kind of superficiality. Postmodernism has eclipsed depth, anxiety, and terror and replaced them with fancy, play, and commitment to surface (1984a:60; 1984b:xviii).

This last note puts one inescapably in mind of Alain Robbe-Grillet's *For a New Novel*, which I have long thought of as one of the most exemplary and revealing manifestos of the postmodern ethos. Although Robbe-Grillet can say that there is no one prescribed path for the novel (1965:14), his book turns out to be a highly provocative prescription for what the novel now ought to be.

We should get away from the idea that there is a dimension of depth or transcendence that is concealed by surface. There is no tragedy because there is no sphere of depth to be—"tragically"—estranged from (23–24, 59–62). Character as a disposition of the individual molded by the past is no longer appropriate in our time of administrative numbers (27–29). No longer is it possible to tell a story with a plot moving toward conclusion and suggesting a coherent universe. In the new novel it would not be possible to reconstruct a non-contradictory order from the jumbled parts of the story (32–33, 151–54). Metaphor carries implications contrary to our experience. In proposing analogies between different kinds of things metaphor implies a higher nature common to all things and thereby suggests transcendence (53–55, 57–58). All of these points come under Robbe-Grillet's rejection of every preestablished order (72–73).

Frank Kermode regards this theoretical contempt for form or order in the arts as a fraud because, he maintains, form is actually inescapable. Look at apparent formlessness clearly enough and organization begins to show through the most chaotic surface (1971:48–49, 59–61).

Postmodern Biblical Theology

Walter Brueggemann

I now want to look at two scholars who propose a biblical theology that is hermeneutical in postmodernist terms and that is highly critical of historical criticism. The first is Walter Brueggemann, whose important *Theology of the Old Testament* (1997) argues a hermeneutical position that is as pertinent for New Testament theology as for Old Testament theology. The second is A. K. M. Adam, who makes the case for New Testament theology. In this chapter I will present their positions and make a few critical comments. The next chapter will give a more comprehensive critique.

Brueggemann has warmly welcomed postmodernism as the end of the modern cultural period introduced by the Enlightenment (1997:61, 103). For him postmodernism is characterized by the pluralism of the context in which we now do interpretation and by the multiplicity of interpretations of any given text. All interpretation is generated and shaped by the desire to advocate an interest held by the interpreter. There is no universal set of assumptions to which one can appeal to justify the claim to have given a right or ultimate interpretation. We have only the text itself and numerous provisional, competing interpretations (61–64).

In this conflictive situation Brueggemann identifies three primary types of Old Testament theology—canonical, liberationist, and historical-critical (1997:62). He is quite critical of the third one, which he sees as an Enlightenment product that has had injurious consequences for the theological interpretation of the Bible. With its objective, scientific, and positivistic assumptions, historical-critical Old Testament theology has produced interpretation that can be characterized as thin, skeptical, and minimalist (61–63, 103, 727–28).

The heart of Brueggemann's criticism of historical-critical Old Testament theology is that with its naturalistic presuppositions it has insisted on explaining everything without reference to any theological claim (1997:727). It has failed to recognize that the text's saturation with the odd, the dense, the hidden, and the inscrutable has the primary intention of speaking about God (104). In sum, Brueggemann seems to regard historical criticism as inherently flawed. It "is problematic in itself" (103).

I would be inclined to argue that historical criticism does not inherently have—and thus need not have—the traits that Brueggemann assigns to it, as I will argue in the next chapter.

Brueggemann must sense that as well, for he states—and I doubt that this is consistent with his claim that historical criticism is problematic in itself—that he does not mean to reject modernist historical criticism out of hand but to be critical of its problems (1997:85, 105). In fact, historical criticism broadly construed— freed from theological skepticism—can help to protect biblical theology from overreaching encroachments by systematic theology (107, 726–28).

The positive side of Brueggemann's critique of historical criticism is his turn to the rhetoric of the Old Testament text itself (1997:64–66, 71, 78). He emphasizes that Old Testament theology is grounded on dramatic-narrative rhetoric, and he is attentive to the prominent role of metaphor and of the artistic imagination more broadly in producing the text of the Old Testament (68–71, 76–77). But Brueggemann's literary-critical hermeneutic seems to contain a tension that is in some way reminiscent of the strain in his posture toward historical criticism.

He calls for a criticism that can engage the density and depth of the text (1997:728–29). But the strictly *critical* dimension in interpretation is undercut by his judgment that the dramatic mode in theology requires the interpreter to stay inside the text and not to venture outside of it. The intention of his postliberal approach is to expound the perspective and claims of the text itself with no attempt to accommodate it to a larger rationality (70, 86). I want to rejoin that an unbroken engagement with the text is appropriate for the stance of faith—or for the aesthetic stance—but the critical stance—whether the criticism be theological, literary, historical, or whatever—requires a distancing from the text. One must stand back to see clearly.

One side of Brueggemann's position tacitly acknowledges that the distanced critical stance is inevitable. That is, he has asserted that all interpretation is shaped by a vested interest of the interpreter (1997:62–63, 73). That necessarily means that the text is always seen in the light of a position that is in some way outside of the text and that the interpreter brings to the text from his or her personal social and theological position and uses as a hermeneutical vantage point. If interpretation is to be thoroughly critical, the interpreter must be self-consciously aware of her or his hermeneutical location and its limitations.

In order to take account of both the importance of existential engagement with the text and the need for conceptual clarity, biblical theology should be understood as a dialectical movement between engagement and critical distance. It is the interpreter's job to show that there is an analogous relationship of some kind between the text and the outside horizon.

In sum, the primary value of postmodernism for Brueggemann is that, in his view, it warrants the biblical interpreter's rejection of a historical criticism that, in Brueggemann's opinion, claims a false objectivity and uses the alleged objective historical knowledge to bracket out the theological significance of the biblical text.

A. K. M. Adam

I take Adam's two books and his editing of two collections of essays by other scholars on various postmodern topics to be a vigorous, forthright, and learned presentation of a hermeneutical and theological position that works under the aegis of postmodernism. Adam borrows three key ideas from Cornel West to give a concise description of postmodernism. Postmodernism is *antifoundational* in that it denies any privileged, unassailable starting point for establishing truth. An interpretation does not derive its authority from its resting on an unassailable, transcendent foundation, such as objective historical accuracy, for there is no such foundation. Authority is rather gained from the interpretation's relationship to the varying local situations—social, political, institutional, religious—of the interpreter. Postmodernism is *antitotalizing* in that it is critical of theories that try to explain the totality of reality. And it is *demystifying* in its effort to show that ideals are characteristically grounded in ideology or economic and political self-interest. Postmodernism shows how problematic it is to validate claims about truth or justice or reality (1995a:4; 1995b:5–16).

Terry Eagleton has observed that postmodernism should not claim that we cannot critically get beyond our local beliefs or interests. To make such a claim is to transform our limited perspectives into the transcendental foundation that postmodernism wants to annihilate (1997:36).

Historical criticism as the indispensable foundation for New Testament theology seems to be the primary target of Adam's critique of modern New Testament theology (1995a:4–5, 122, 143). But his questioning of the validity of historical criticism manifests a certain ambivalence, similar to Brueggemann's. On the one hand, he states that he is simply arguing for the relativization of the role of historical criticism and for the recognition of the validity of other hermeneutical approaches (1995a:2, 143). And he does give tentative, pragmatic, and non-principled support to the historical approach (1995a:159, 180, 204, 209). But his real position comes out when he asserts that the perceived need for a historical foundation rests not on the nature of interpretation or the nature of New Testament theology itself but on the modern ethos with its stress on point of origin, chronological determination, novel interpretation, and technical expertise. Historical New Testament theology is a social and institutional necessity—the scholarly guild demands it—not a methodological or theological necessity (1995a:1, 142, 209). History-based New Testament theology is only for those who have not been able to extricate themselves from modernism.

Is Adam then advocating the replacement of a modern, history-based New Testament theology with a new and improved postmodern approach? He denies that he is. To do so would only be to fall into the modern web of trying to get somewhere by surpassing someone else with something new (1995a:2, 143, 166). But the effort to achieve a new and better formulation, which Adam programmatically rejects, inserts itself deconstructively into Adam's discourse and may be seen in three claims or moves.

1. The blindness and other problems of New Testament theology over two centuries are directly related to its modernity (1995a:2, 49, 86–87, 122, 124, 141). But these problems have

been correctly diagnosed and exposed by postmodern thinkers (113, 143).

2. The antifoundational position of postmodernism, which Adam clearly advocates in *What Is Postmodern Biblical Criticism?* (1995b:xi, 1, 4–6, 8, 76), is the criterion for his critique of historical criticism in *Making Sense of New Testament Theology* (1995a:4–5, 178–79, 186).

3. The problems inherent in modern New Testament theology cannot be corrected by fine tuning. A change of course away from the procedures and criteria of modernity needs to be made (1995a:168).

Adam, however, cannot acknowledge that he is in fact advocating a new and better—postmodern—New Testament theology, for if he did, that would make it explicit that his position is simply another stage of modernism—giving a new and surpassing formulation.

For Adam, the task of New Testament theology is to make sense of the New Testament. Sense is not something that a text has but something that an interpreter ascribes to it in the light of categories already familiar to the interpreter. New Testament theology begins with a sense that one makes of the New Testament; one then states this in a different way. It is, however, not necessary to seek the original meaning (1995a:169–71, 180).

But Adam does affirm other possible critical, ordering criteria for testing the validity of New Testament theology. Among then are: orientation to the canon, the rubrics of systematic theology, ethical concerns, aesthetic judgment, and political and liberationist interests (1995a:3–4, 182–95).

I agree with Adam that the role of historical criticism should be relativized in the face of legitimate claims made by other hermeneutical approaches. And I do not believe that biblical texts have only one original and authoritative meaning. But I do have two critical questions to pose, the first to be engaged in this chapter and the second in the next.

Does the New Testament itself really justify the claim that historical inquiry is neither a methodological nor theological necessity for New Testament theology? And does postmodernism in any global way justify the claim that historical materials may be treated by a nonhistorical method?

I believe that the necessity for historical-critical interpretation resides ultimately, not in the ethos of modernism, but in the New Testament claims about the nature of revelation. For the New Testament God is manifested in concrete, specific, particular events, words, and images. Only historical investigation enables us to get some handle on the particularity of the vehicles of revelation. Our historical reconstructions will never be completely certain, but apart from some sense of the particularity of the New Testament message, we will use it as a sounding board for our own ideas—though all interpretation expresses the interpreter's pre-understanding to some degree.

Adam is aware of this problem and tries to solve it by taking otherness and particularity as the same thing and stating that any method can show respect for otherness (1995a:181). But otherness and particularity are not necessarily identical; and it is doubtful whether the particularity of a New Testament text or motif can be demonstrated other than by comparing it to other New Testament phenomena and to the larger history-of-religions and cultural context.

Adam faults modern historical-critical New Testament theologians for maintaining that they alone have the authority to make truth-claims about what Jesus said while rejecting the conclusions of those without scholarly credentials (1995a:144–45). This way of putting it is a troubling confusion of the issue, for it passes over the fact that actually two levels of truth are involved. One is historical truth. Historical reconstruction cannot attain objectively certain truth about the past—what actually happened. It must deal with lesser and greater probabilities. But only those with scholarly expertise are competent to assess the complex evidence and reach conclusions about the probabilities of what the historical Jesus actually said.

The other level of truth is theological truth. The historian, as historian, does not have the authority to limit the possible theological significance of what he or she thinks Jesus probably said to a meaning rigidly circumscribed by the original context. Theological truth depends upon theological reflection on the contribution that a probable saying of Jesus might make to our understanding of the interrelationships among God, humankind, and the world. And that reflection is shaped by the religious and social location of the interpreter.

Stanley Hauerwas

Although he has sometimes been taken to be a postmodernist and has some sympathies with the movement, Hauerwas disclaims the connection. He thinks that postmodernism is too comfortable a story for alienated intellectuals, doubts that such a thing as a coherent postmodern position exists, and believes that Christians should not side with postmodernism—because Christians have a stake in history (Hauerwas 1999:107–9, 115, 120 nn. 2 and 5). This last claim, however, does not prompt him to recognize that taking history seriously requires critical historiography—historical criticism of the Bible.

In his 1993 book Hauerwas programmatically resists the higher critical method for studying Scripture (7). He believes that people cannot rightly understand Scripture "on their own" but only when they submit to the mediation and authority of the community that has been morally and spiritually transformed (1993:9, 15–17). Historical critics mistakenly believe, as do fundamentalists, that the biblical text has an original objective meaning (one not dependent on the community) that can be recovered in its context by objective description (18, 33–34). This alleged objectivity conceals from the critics the political character of their interpretation, the privileging of the constituency they serve, that is, the rational individual who believes that truth (including Christian truth) can be known without initiation into the community of the transformed (35).

Hauerwas has failed to engage those biblical theologians who have acknowledged the kinds of flaws and limitations that he has observed and who have devised interpretative strategies to disarm the problems while maintaining the necessity for historical criticism.

John Dominic Crossan

The work of Crossan presents an alternative to both Adam and Hauerwas. Crossan attributes to himself a postmodern sensibility and also strongly affirms the necessity of historical Jesus research—for Catholic (orthodox) Christianity but not for gnostic Christianity (1999:283, 301). His understandings of postmodernism and historical scholarship closely parallel each other. By postmodernism he means interactivism. Past and present must interact with each other, each challenging the other in a fair and equal manner (1999:304). History is not the same as story but rather has a real past. It is the past reconstructed interactively by the present through argued evidence in public discourse (1999:284). Since the past is reconstructed in light of the present and the present of historians is always changing, history is always changing, and the scholar's reconstructions must be ever redone (1999:306).

In a concise statement from the last section of his 1994 book on Jesus Crossan declares: "Christian belief is (1) an act of faith (2) in the historical Jesus (3) as the manifestation of God" (1994:200). The import of this pregnant formulation is that historical investigation is ingredient in Crossan's theological project. That is, the object of Christian faith is in significant part constituted by historical reconstruction (1991:426; 1994:200), and Crossan has given extended attention to historical context and method (1991:xxvii–xxxiv, 1–224, 427–66).

For Crossan there are three reasons that compel scholarly historical reconstruction (1999:285):

1. The historical reason. Jesus and his companions are historical figures who are simply there and can be studied by anyone with the appropriate competence (1999:286).
2. The ethical reason. The gospel is not composed entirely of story, parable, and theology but has always claimed a historical basis. Thus we have an ethical responsibility to distinguish historical from theological statements (1999:290).

3. The theological reason. This for Crossan is the most important reason for historical Jesus research, and he bases it on the normative value of the nature—content and form—of the canonical Gospels (293, 301). For these biographical Gospels the incarnation is truly, and not apparently, an enfleshment, and it is the importance of Jesus' body that makes him historically important (300–1).

The canonical Gospels are normative precisely in that they configure a dialectic between the Palestinian Jesus of the late twenties of the first century and the present of the Gospel writers and their communities, who lived in faith in the risen Christ. It is always a dialectic between historical-Jesus-then and risen-Jesus-now. This interaction must be repeated again and again throughout Christian history. There is for believers one Jesus—the historical Jesus as risen (301–2).

The New Testament itself disqualifies any theology that is not historical-critical. Critical historical inquiry is not a dispensable option. This claim is grounded on the fact that the New Testament is composed of documents that are *historical* in nature (see chapter 7). This history is *particular* in content, and the New Testament assigns great theological value to *this* particularity. Therefore, *critical* analysis is necessary to clarify the nature of this particularity in its discontinuities and continuities with other particularities in its context. This is needed in order to diminish the tendency to assimilate the Bible unduly to the interests of any present reader.

7

Reprise: History, Hermeneutics, and Postmodernism

History

New Testament theologians need to be reminded that historical investigation—like the other human sciences—is situated in a tissue of uncertainty (Cousins 1989:127–28). But postmodernism gives no global warrant to the belief that historical materials can be legitimately treated in a nonhistorical way.

The New Testament is composed of documents that are historical at least in the broad and nontechnical sense that they refer—directly or indirectly—to events or situations that really happened, or are believed to have happened, but are no longer directly accessible to perception (see White 1989b:295, 297). Is it only the *modernist* intellectual climate that prompts us to be critically reflective about the status and interrelationships of events, concepts, intentions, and ideologies of the past? I think not. While there are different positions within postmodernism, we can identify important (nontheological) postmodern theorists who, while they have renounced the expectation of "objective" historical knowledge, by no means regard critical research into the real past as merely optional.

Louis Montrose formulated the now-famous chiastic statement that historical study is reciprocally concerned with the historicity of texts and the textuality of history. The historicity of texts means that all texts are conditioned by a specific social and cultural setting. The textuality of history means that we have no access to a lived past except through the mediation of the figurations of language (Montrose 1989:20).

For Hayden White the narrative moment in historical scholarship entails the same linguistic figurations and rhetorical strategies that imaginative writers employ. The narrative form is not an empty container to hold the contents gleaned from research; rather the narrative *form* has a *content* of its own, which is the meaning of the plot that the historian imposes on the events narrated in order to interpret them. The same set of events has a different content dependent on whether it is plotted as a tragedy, a romance, a comedy, or a satire. But White maintains that historical scholarship also contains as a necessary moment the research effort intended to discover the truth about the past (1978:58–59, 62, 70; 1989a:21, 24–25; 1989b:295; 1990:xi, 2, 4–5, 43–47).

Hans Kellner sets forth the rhetorical or constructed character of our knowledge of the past in his claims that historical scholarship is a matter of getting the story crooked, not straight, and that the rhetorical discourse is one of the *sources* for history writing. The historian's employment of metaphors such as life cycles, roots, seeds, flow, gears, crossroads, chains, and so on is a matter of explanation, not just of adornment (1989:vii–viii, 7–8). Kellner points to the debate among historians about which of the two moments—research into the facts and narrative production—is the causal infrastructure and which is the resultant superstructure. He seems to hold that at every stage of historical understanding, documentary evidence and literary construction are reciprocally dependent on each other, but he obviously does not relinquish the moment of research into the past (10, 328–33).

In his discussion of the effacement of history in postmodernism Fredric Jameson states that in poststructuralist linguistic theory the past as referent has been bracketed and then effaced altogether, leaving us with nothing but texts. But interestingly Jameson substantiates this assertion with references, not to the works of historians, but to historical novels (1984b:65–66, 68–71). For his own part he declares that if a work of art is not to sink to the level of sheer decoration we must reconstruct some initial situation out of which it emerges (1984b:58). And more broadly he calls for a renewal of historical analysis within postmodernism and a reexamination of its political and ideological functionality (1989:372).

Eagleton draws the conclusion that postmodernism is not opposed to history—to historicizing or to the scholarly effort to understand phenomena in their context. What it does oppose is a story-shaped entity called History possessed of an immanent meaning and purpose that is presently unfolding itself around us (1997:30–33).

The New Testament is a set of historical documents. Since postmodernism neither requires nor warrants treating the New Testament in a nonhistorical way, we are prompted to ask what is the real reason that some postmodern New Testament theologians are so captivated by the belief that historical criticism may be taken as a merely dispensable option. In exactly what sense might historical criticism be seen to be unfriendly to theological interpretation?

The answers to these questions probably vary from case to case, but whatever the answer, N. T. Wright makes one interesting suggestion. The pietistic tradition in the church has institutionalized certain ways of reading Scripture that are strangely similar to some strands in postmodernism. The predecessor of deconstruction is the pietistic tradition that chooses not to read the Bible in light of its historical particularity, and it makes this choice in order that the be-all and the end-all of its meaning might be what the text says to *me, now* (Wright 1992:60). Could it be that the negative evaluation of historical criticism does not emanate ultimately from an allegiance to postmodernism? It rather results from the belief that the requirement to reflect on how the Bible's *distanced particularity* might meld with our present particularity is an impediment to making the Bible *immediately* available to us *now*.

To take this shortcut actually diminishes the authority of the Bible by making the readers' location primary, and the use of postmodernism to support the choice may bring in a load of factors hostile to a Christian worldview. On the other hand, historical criticism positively undergirds the theological project. N. T. Wright, again, points to the paradox that while the Enlightenment began in part as a critique of orthodox Christianity, it can function and often has functioned to recall Christianity to its necessary roots in genuine history (1992:60; 1996:661–62). It needs to be said further that critical study of the historical past treats the actual past in its particularity as *other* than our own situation. This acknowledges our distance from the past and gives expression to our sense of living in a chronological succession, our sense of moving from a past through the present into a future, our sense of the narrative quality of existence. If we abandon the kind of historical investigation and reflection that sustain our existential sense of historical existence, then we undermine the existential possibility itself.

Fredric Jameson describes conceptually the loss of chronological awareness in (some) postmodernism. If the subject has lost the capacity to remember and anticipate, to organize past and future in coherent experience, then how can her or his cultural productions result in anything but "heaps of fragments" and a practice that is randomly heterogeneous and fragmentary (1984b:71)? A more poetic angle of vision is turned on the same condition in some lines spoken by the character Pozzo in Samuel Beckett's *Waiting for Godot*: "The blind have no notion of time. . . . One day I went blind, one day we'll go deaf, one day we were born, one day we shall die, the same day, the same second, is that not enough for you? They give birth astride the grave" (Beckett 1954:55, 57). All times are collapsed into the same vacant second, day, or year. Existentially speaking this is the extreme end of the road that we start down when we choose not to treat the past as really past and other but assimilate it radically to our present interests. New Testament theology should not go there.

If the historical sense has been lost in some forms of postmodernism, that does not mean, as we have seen, that postmodernism as a whole has rejected it.

God

Barry Harvey has declared that it is ironic and wasteful for believers to defend modern ways of thinking, which are under serious

attack, when modernity in many respects has sought to undermine the Christian tradition (2000:7). This might be supported
by Wesley A. Kort's argument that modernity tended to read nature,
history, and literature—but finally not the Bible—as scripture
(Kort 1996:37). But then significant aspects of postmodernism are
no friendlier to a hermeneutical New Testament theology than is
modernism. Kort's description of postmodernism, which he
praises in certain respects, might support that contention. To read
a text as though it were scripture is to understand the text as having the power to become the site of a transformative event (26,
35). The weakness of postmodernism is that it has characteristically declined to read anything as scripture. And it has attributed
so much power to the reader to determine meaning that the text is
deprived of the capacity to put the reader in question (20, 66–70).

I should like to question postmodernism about its orientation
toward the most elemental theological theme—God or the transcendent. Of course, not all postmodern Biblical scholars and theologians are atheistic, but that tendency is there and can be made
visible by reference to Jacques Derrida. Derrida has stated that he
never used the word "postmodern" and that he deemed the concept to be unreliable, obscure, and useless (Derrida 1999:181–82).
In fact he claims to be a rationalist, a phenomenologist, and a
man of the Enlightenment (1999:75). His influence on postmodernism, however, is strongly evident and is often noted (Sherwood
2000:72).

For Derrida, a rupture has occurred in our world, and that
rupture is language's invasion of our universal realm of problems. Everything has become discourse. Because this rupture has
occurred, it is necessary for us to think through its entailment—
to recognize that there is no center (1970:249). What then is center and how does the universal invasion of language undo it?

Center is presence, the state of something being fully present in
itself. It functions as a fixed, unchanging origin, as a governing
principle, as form—all of which restrict the free play of meaning.
Center makes something absolutely what it is, self-identical (Derrida 1970:247–49; 1980:12–13; 1979b:108).

Language disassembles the presence or self-identity of center in that language is a system of differences. Derrida plays upon the two senses of the French verb "to differ" (*différer*), which he combines by means of the new spelling of the noun *differance*. To differ means to be distinct or other, but it also suggests to defer or delay (Derrida 1979b:129). Traditionally, the linguistic sign has been understood as composed of a signifier (vehicle of meaning, sound, or writing) and a signified (mental construct). But for Derrida the signified is a signifier because they both express meaning in the same way. The sign as a whole has no meaning in itself but expresses meaning in its *difference* or otherness from other signs. Thus it means by referring to another, and that other means by referring to another still and so on in an endless chain of references. Thus meaning is perpetually deferred and not present (1979b:139–41; 1980:7, 73).

The invasion of language affects everything. Human consciousness or subjectivity is never identical with itself because it is shaped by language (Derrida 1979b:146–48) in its differences. And we have access to the flesh and bone of "real" existence outside of language only by means of the text. That is what Derrida means by "there is nothing outside the text" (1980:158–59). Thus all that we experience is caught up in the referential chain of differences and is not present to itself but is rather deferred.

The character of language and reality as constituted by differences invites deconstruction as a way of interpreting and understanding. If nothing is ever fully present in itself, we are prompted to look for the other that makes something different from itself. Deconstruction affirms that when discourse attempts to exclude what would be logically incompatible (the other) and to push it to the outside, that outside reinserts itself, probably in a subordinate position. Deconstructive interpretation reverses the hierarchy of meanings, making the dominant low and the subordinate high. Then it develops a displaced or reinscribed concept that would have been impossible within the old arrangement (Derrida 1979a:97; 1982:91–95; Leavey 1982:50–51).

We may illustrate with Derrida's deconstruction of the "gift." Derrida's analysis assumes that giving a gift intends a benefit for the receiver but no benefit for or self-interest on the part of the giver. That is what a gift is. Once the gift is given and is known as such, it ceases to be a gift, however, for the receiver becomes obligated to the giver and the latter becomes self-congratulated. Therefore, it is impossible for the gift to be present in itself as a gift (Derrida 1999:59–61).

Now we can address the specifically theological issue. According to Derrida, in the traditional view of the linguistic sign the signified (mental content) is free from the signifier and from the unending chain of differential reference. This closely parallels the notion of divinity. In fact "the sign and divinity have the same place and time of birth" (1980:13–14). God is by definition the transcendent signified, separate from signifiers and from the play of differences, pure intelligibility, an absolute logos (rationality), infinite creative subjectivity, present to itself (1980:7, 10–14, 18, 20, 53, 71). Since for Derrida there is no signified that is present to itself and not defined by a chain of references (1979b:139–40), there is no God. He speaks of the death of God—though not in a wholly undialectical way (1998:12, 43)—and says of himself, "I quite rightly pass for an atheist" (Caputo and Scanlon 1999:1). Whether Derrida's definition of God fits the biblical God is another question.

I turn now to two notable postmodern scholars who theologize out of the death of God and the end of transcendence and who reveal Derrida's influence. Mark C. Taylor interprets the experience of the death of God as a non-revealing disaster, a nonevent, an ending that never ends and in which nothing happens. This entails the subversion of the self and the incapacity of language to refer to anything (1990a:49–50, 53, 56, 58–59, 62–65, 67–69). Thomas J. J. Altizer, on the other hand, interprets the death of God as the full advent of apocalypse, the revelation of total grace (Altizer 1990:88, 92–94, 97, 99, 101, 105). But when one learns from Altizer that total grace brings total death, the end of eternal life, total silence, and total nothingness (101, 102, 106–8), it becomes difficult to tell the difference between disaster and apocalypse. In fact, Taylor performed a clever deconstruction of Altizer's position showing that disaster is inherent in apocalypse.

Apocalypse, says Taylor, is a vision about (coming) visions. But the future manifestation is interminably and endlessly deferred. The space of this delay is the time of the disaster. In this non-occurrence nothing happens. The disastrous end neither is nor is not; the end is never present nor is it simply absent. There is always nothing left to say, but we say it again and again, endlessly. (Taylor 1990b:138–42, 147).

I should now like to return to Derrida with the suggestion that he is not as nihilistic as (some of) his heirs and that his atheism is not as unambiguously assertive as it may appear to be. It is not the case, as has sometimes been said, that Derrida seems to break completely with religious tradition (Ingraffia 1995:232). Derrida states that he is not an enemy of religion, that he is in fact interested in Christianity and in the gift in the Christian sense, and that he is interested in Christian theology (1998:7; 1999:57–58, 67).

To become more specific, Derrida offers an interesting discussion of religion as being composed of two sources or foci: (1) the experience of faith, belief, trust, commitment; (2) the experience of the sacred. These two are often associated, but they are distinct and heterogeneous, and one may exist without connection to the other (1998:30–33, 36). He then asks a probing question about revelation. Is revealability (the possibility that enables revelation) more originary than the actual event or manifestation of revelation and hence independent of all religion? Or is the event of revelation the manifestation of revealability? Derrida does not decide between the two but regards the indecisive oscillation between them (event and possibility) as something to be respected (1998:6, 15–16, 21; 1999:73).

Still more provocative is Derrida's distinction between messianism and messianicity. The former maintains the historical advent of an actual, historical messianic figure. The latter would be the opening to the future or to the coming of the other as the advent of justice. It would come without prophetic prefiguration and tear history apart. Thus messianicity is unconnected to a specific messiah, but it belongs to a faith that has no dogma (1998:17–18).

The actual coming of a messiah is as impossible as the presence of the gift. But it is precisely the impossibility that keeps one desiring, dreaming, questioning toward the future. Thus for Derrida impossibility is not a negative concept (1999:72).

Does Derrida's position on revealability and messianicity point to belief in God or at least to the philosophical viability of belief in God? Possibly. There is perhaps a God of the future, but as soon as you think you have the criteria for identifying the true God, faith has ended and God has left (Derrida 1999:133). According to Caputo and Scanlon, Derrida does not dismiss God per se but insists on a general openness to an otherness without name or identity, indeterminate and undefined (1999:13). The impossibility of God's or the messiah's ever showing is what keeps desire alive and the future open. Thus impossibility is not the gloomy end but the beginning. The presence of God for Derrida is neither historical incarnation nor mystical union, but neither is it atheism. The presence of God means God's coming and the faith, hope, and love of the future that this coming elicits. God is neither simply present nor absent (Caputo 1999:186, 199).

However, another concept of Derrida, perhaps his ultimate concept, seems to make his possible theological affirmation still more ambiguous. Derrida borrows from Plato the concept of *chōra* but says that he interprets it against Plato (1999:73). For Plato the "all" is composed of three categories. First, there is the pattern of intelligible, changeless, unbegotten, imperishable, invisible ideas. Second, there is the copy of this pattern—created, visible, in motion, coming into being in a certain place, and then perishing. Third, there is the substrate space—*chōra*—a form obscure and dim that is the everlasting and invisible receptacle that provides a place for the copies that come into being and then perish. *Chōra* itself is lacking in all specific forms or qualities so that it can receive the imprint of the eternal ideas. But *chōra* is inferior to the pattern of ideas (*Timaeus* 49A–52D).

For Derrida *chōra* does not happen, give, or desire. But it is the universal space, the groundless ground, the possibility that *makes* place for all that takes place. But it does not *give* place. In fact it is indifferent to what happens and is the element of resistance in all that takes place. It is thus what negates presence; it is the non-being, the non-thing in any thing, the impossible, that stimulates hope for a future of justice (Derrida 1999:67, 76–77).

Chōra is prior to all else, more ancient that all oppositions. It is neither Being, nor "beyond Being," nor the Good, nor God, nor Man, nor History. It is heterogeneous to all the processes of history and religion; it never presents itself as such but is the utterly faceless other—nothing—no being—nothing present (Derrida 1998:19–21; 1999:67). In the end *chōra*—nonbeing—is more originary than God.

The eschatology of Derrida is probably closer to the New Testament than is that of Altizer and Taylor and is a more fruitful hermeneutical vantage point. But it cannot be said that postmodernism is globally more congenial to the theology of the New Testament than modernism is. Nor can it be maintained that modernism is more hostile to the New Testament than postmodernism is. In fact, if we take the following four defining features that Adam used to characterize modernism, the latter is seen to be a development and formalizing of certain New Testament motifs. These four modernist traits need not be regarded as incompatible with a proper New Testament theology nor as responsible for the "blindness" of modern New Testament theology.

(1) Modernism is committed to the new, to the overthrowing of traditional canons, to rebellion against past interpretations, which are seen as inadequate (Adam 1995a:10–11). But then so is the New Testament—since it offers a new covenant to replace the old (Luke 22:20; 2 Cor 3:6; Heb 8:8, 13; 9:15). The antitheses of the Sermon on the Mount (Matt 5:21-48) replace an old interpretation of the law ("you have heard") with a new one ("but I say"). Paul thought the Jewish interpretation of the law as calling for works to be wrong and his new interpretation that the law calls for faith to be right (Rom 9:30—10:8). According to the Johannine Jesus, the Jews believed that Moses in giving Israel manna gave them the bread from heaven (John 6:31-32). But Jesus corrects them with the new claim that Scripture refers to him (5:39-40, 45-46) and that he him-

self is the bread from heaven (6:33, 35, 38). There is more to come that is unimaginable now (John 14:25-26; 16:12-14).

(2) For modernism all situations are time conditioned; thus the passage of time automatically puts distance between the past and the present (Adam 1995a:12). The New Testament does not reflect on this issue in a theoretical way. But the truth of this claim is indirectly and practically demonstrated in that the different theological messages of various New Testament texts can be accounted for by the fact that they were written in different theological, social, and cultural situations.

(3) Modernism then asserts that the only way to deal with the gap between past and present is by the application of the correct scholarly method (Adam 1995a:12). The drive toward methodological accuracy and correctness is anticipated by the concern of the New Testament to get the theology right. Not just anything goes. Paul, for example, is astonished that the Galatians have turned so quickly from his true gospel to another false one (Gal 1:6, 9). And Paul makes methodological assumptions as well as theological judgments. The form of his letters is congruent with the rhetorical expectations of his time. A more material point is that Paul's preference for the latent over the surface meaning of a text shows him to be—as Frank Kermode implies (1979:x–xi, 1–2)—a member of the guild of professional scholars. And Paul used midrashic and allegorical methods for eliciting that latent sense (Via 1997:78–90).

(4) For modernism the methodological task is carried out by a guild of scholarly experts who place themselves above simple lay people (Adam 1995a:13, 44–47, 86). This distinction is foreshadowed in the New Testament. Paul calls on all Christians to be transformed by the renewal of their minds (Rom 12:1-3). The word for "mind" means the power to make critical judgments, the ability to test and differentiate. But some believers—not all—are given a special gift of wisdom and knowledge and are called to be teachers (Rom 12:6-8; 1 Cor 12:4-11, 27-31). All gifts are important, but they are not identical. The position is similar in Hebrews 5:11-14; 6:1-3.

There are still fruitful hermeneutical vantage points in modernism—and cultural epochs are seen to be not always sharply distinguished.

Is Postmodernism Really Here?

Up to this point I have generally adopted the assumption of postmodernism's champions that we do in fact live in the postmodern era. Postmodernism has articulated important positions, some of which I agree with. But I doubt that New Testament theology should sail programmatically under a banner called "postmodernism," and I decline to identify myself as *being* a postmodernist for the following reasons.

1. One is the difficulty of defining the postmodern mind and situation, of determining whether it has a coherence that constitutes an identity distinguishable from modernism; and thus we have the problem of ascertaining whether it actually exists. We see this acknowledged, for example, in the work of Hassan (1987:xv, 29, 53, 84–88, 167–68), in Robert P. Scharlemann's introduction to his symposium on postmodern theology (1990:1), and in Eagleton's political critique (1997:viii–ix).

We have already observed Derrida's disinclination to use the term postmodernism or to consider it useful. According to Kermode any development in "postmodernism" beyond modernism is merely marginal. The postmodern attempt to abolish form is only an extension of the older modernism's program to give form a new researched look (1971:59–61). Reiss holds that serious tensions within modernism point to the need for a new kind of discourse; but he maintains that postmodernism is only a potentiality whose actuality awaits the passage of time. Reiss places alleged "postmodern" thinkers such as Paul de Man, Stanley Fish, Geoffrey H. Hartman, Jacques Derrida, and others within the discourse of modernism (Reiss 1982:378–83). Calinescu argues that postmodernism has developed enough distinctive features to be regarded as a full-fledged "face of modernity," on a par with modernism (1987:265, 312). At the same time he recognizes that the two share common features and suggests that postmodernism is not so much a new reality or mental structure as a perspective from which to ask questions about modernity (269, 279). And postmodernism is still a face of *modernity*.

Fredric Jameson recognizes the extensive heterogeneity of the cultural expressions that followed the exhaustion of high modernism, and he also acknowledges that there is a question as to whether the break *between* these recent postmodern phenomena and late modernism is any more definitive than the changes that occurred *within* the modernist movement (1984b:53–54; 1989:373). Jameson then looks for a unifying principle that will establish a global identity for postmodernism while accommodating a range of very different subordinate features. He finds this defining unity in what he calls a dominant cultural logic that can distinguish postmodernism from modernism. Any number of individual features attributed to postmodernism may be found in earlier periods, but what is different in postmodernism is the positioning of *cultural* production in the economic system of late capitalism. Modernism was canonized and academically institutionalized. But aesthetic production today has become integrated into commodity production generally. Aesthetic innovation is simply an aspect of the frantic economic urgency to produce ever fresh waves of more novel-seeming goods (1984a:56–57). If there are those who do not believe that the almost complete commodification of cultural products—including scholarly knowledge—is a present reality, all they need to do to be disabused of their illusion is to attend an annual meeting of the Society of Biblical Literature and the American Academy of Religion.

I am not, however, convinced that Jameson's dominant cultural logic, if real, alleviates the uncertainties about who and what belong to "postmodernism." I offer a very few examples. Jean-François Lyotard seems to identify himself with postmodernism, but Jameson (1984a:xvi) in his foreword to Lyotard's book holds that Lyotard has not really made a fundamental break with high modernism (Jameson 1984a:xvi). Hassan interprets Hemingway as belonging both to modernism and postmodernism (1987:29, 45).

While Jameson takes existentialism to exemplify modernism
(1984b:53), Hassan places it in postmodernism (1987:29). Both
proponents (as we have seen) and opponents (Ingraffia 1995:6–10,
14, 228, 233) of postmodernism have seen the rejection of divine
transcendence as one of its most characteristic features. Edgar V.
McKnight, on the other hand, seems to associate the subversion of
transcendence with modernism (1994:331). Perhaps these and
other such uncertainties rest on the fact that we are too close to
the period beginning about 1960 to have enough perspective to
know whether this period has a distinguishing identity.

Timothy Reiss's view of the nature of cultural epochs is useful
for our problem. In any cultural era there will be one dominant
discourse for explaining things, but it will be accompanied by a
dominant eclipsed or hidden discourse. A situation may be
reached in which the dominant discourse fails to handle pressing
problems and is seriously questioned. Thus the concealed discourse rises to greater prominence. The dominant discourse of
modernity has maintained that reason can attain objective knowledge of the external world in order to control and manipulate the
latter. The hidden discourse recognizes, on the contrary, that the
human view of the world is necessarily dependent on perspective,
not objective, and that the reality to be interpreted should be
respected and listened to rather than having our rationality
imposed upon it. "Postmodernism" then would be the emergence
of modernism's own hidden discourse into a role of greater
impact and consequence (Reiss 1982:11, 21, 37, 378–83; Calinescu
1987:272–73; Eagleton 1997:21).

In sum, I doubt the wisdom of placing New Testament theology under the aegis of postmodernism because of my skepticism
about whether the phenomenon has a real existence. I prefer to
deal with specific issues, such as textuality, the reader's role in creating meaning, historiography, and transcendence rather than
with a named cultural epoch. That name almost inevitably, and
whether or not it is intended, takes on some kind of normative
status. Calinescu has observed that the loose and widespread use
of the term "postmodernism" has enhanced the dubious "aura"

that has come to surround it—an aura that has bedazzled a number of biblical scholars (1987:266).

2. My second composite reason for declining to identify myself as a postmodernist is that certain themes characteristically attributed to postmodernism I take to be simply wrong and fallacious. I mention two.

(a) The recurrent rejection of divine transcendence in postmodernism is quite incompatible with a Christian worldview. Temma Berg, writing from a candidly non-Christian point of view, doubts that a Christian can read the New Testament in a poststructuralist or deconstructive—postmodern—way. Her reasoning is that a Christian reads the New Testament to affirm his or her faith and must end up maintaining the transcendence of God and the divinity of Christ, while postmodernism calls for a continuing radical questioning that rules out the kind of foundation Christians need (1989:190–92, 196).

Berg writes as if transcendence and Christology have single, univocal meanings for Christianity when in point of fact each is subject to a spectrum of interpretations. But if a Christian came to the point of renouncing any kind of belief in a transcendent God or in the eschatological significance of Jesus, he or she in honesty would have to renounce the faith. If postmodernism *requires* interpretations and positions that are absolutely and unqualifiedly indeterminable, then one would have to choose between being a Christian and being a postmodernist. But it should be recognized that Berg's absolute indeterminacy is just as foundational—impossible to surpass—as the Christian's transcendence or Christology.

(b) The widespread tendency in postmodernism to reject what Robbe-Grillet, for example, called "every pre-established order" (1965:73) I regard as also wrong. I agree that the order of the world, or of texts, is not obvious or hard and fast. And I agree that the interpreters of texts and of our experience of the world are constructing meaning—and truth—and that there is a plurality of possible legitimate interpretations. But in view of the impossibility of separating subject and object in perception, I do not agree that the subject's interpretative constructions are without any direction whatsoever from the world out there. I have tried to argue this philosophically elsewhere (Via 1985:209–22).

In the preface to his *Handbook of Postmodern Biblical Interpretation,* Adam refers to those who resist postmodernism as fearful and anxious members of an uncomprehending rear guard (2000:viii–ix). That is probably an apt description of some opponents of postmodernism, but there are others to whom it in no way applies. I mention two critics of postmodernism—the first tacit and the second overt—who can hardly be called anxious or uncomprehending.

In the extensive Index of Persons in Jacques Barzun's magisterial history of Western culture from 1500 to the present there is not a single citation of any of the postmodern thinkers discussed in Adam's *Handbook of Postmodern Biblical Interpretation* (2000). Nor is there any discussion of postmodernism as such although there are a couple of passing allusions to it (Barzun 2000:xvii, 733). However, when one reads Barzun's discussion of the period from about 1920 to the 1990s, one may well draw the conclusion that postmodernism is the referent of the last word in the title of Barzun's book—*From Dawn to Decadence.*

When a *New York Times* interviewer asked Richard Rorty (1997)—a distinguished philosopher who is often regarded as an advocate of postmodernism—what he thought was the Most Overrated Idea, Rorty replied:

> The first thing that comes to mind is post-modernism. It's one of these terms that has been used so much that nobody has the foggiest idea what it means. It means one thing in philosophy, another thing in architecture and nothing in literature. It would be nice to get rid of it. It isn't exactly an idea; it's a word that pretends to stand for an idea. Or maybe the idea that one ought to get rid of is that there is any need to get beyond modernity.

In summary, it would be more circumspect of New Testament theology to engage the issues raised by "postmodernism" than to accord to it some kind of global allegiance—as if it were a coherent view of the world with an identity of its own.

8

Conclusions

In surveying the enterprise of New Testament theology I have focused largely on three hermeneutical methods or approaches: historical criticism, literary criticism, and existential interpretation. These three, it seems to me, address the four factors in any interpretive situation that must be taken account of if interpretation is to be as fully adequate as it might be.

Historical criticism deals with (1) the context and its impact on the text, including the questioning of putative factual material in the text. Literary criticism attends to the (2) content and (3) structure or form of the text—two dimensions that may be distinguished for analysis but are not separated in actuality. We are talking about content-as-structured, or informed-content. Existential interpretation also deals with (2) the content of the text, the divine-human interaction, but may pay little attention to the impact of form on meaning. Existential interpretation with its affirmation of the inescapability of the hermeneutical circle, the legitimate effect of the interpreter's posture and pre-understanding on the outcome of interpretation, acknowledges (4) the creative and constitutive role of the reader in the interpretive process.

Before proceeding I should acknowledge—selectively—the objection that some will raise to my implication that content or meaning may be attributed to texts. Stanley Fish has claimed that no meaning is embedded in a text and that its formal features are the creation of the reader's interpretive acts, guided by an interpretive community (Fish 1980a:172, 176–79; 1980b:12–14). Jeffrey Stout believes that the question of the meaning of a text neither requires nor deserves an answer and that the mention of meaning should be eliminated, even if meaning exists (Stout 1982:1, 10). Stephen Fowl, building on Stout, has also argued that texts do not have meaning or ideologies (in the sense of conceptual frameworks related to a range of social, political, and material practices) (Fowl 1995).

To this position I have several responses: (1) Fish's argument unravels because he is unable or unwilling to say what an interpretation is an interpretation *of* (1980a:177)—if the reader creates the meaning of the text. (2) The words on the page are not just meaningless signs (ciphers) waiting for a reader to give them meaning. A text or utterance is a particular manifestation of a language system, in which words and structures have a meaning given by the society that uses it (de Saussure 1966:1, 4–18; Scholes 1985:152, 154, 159–62). (3) Fowl's argument is not a real argument but a series of illustrations of the non-self-evident assumption that because texts have multiple different interpretations they have no meaning. (4) I do not believe that a text has just one original and definitive meaning that is the only proper goal of interpretation. A text will rather generate a multiplicity of justifiable meanings. But it also has a potentiality for meaning that imposes some limits on the range of legitimate interpretations (Iser 1980:9, 18–19, 21–27, 36–38, 107, 141). If the claim in the preceding paragraph were to be taken seriously, then any text whatsoever could be used to justify any ideological agenda whatsoever.

To return now to the carrying out of New Testament theology, any theological interpretation of the New Testament that actualizes all four of the interpretive factors is on the right track. But to state my position in this broad and general way is an oversimplification, for each of the four factors is contested from within by those who address it, with the result that each of these types of interpretation presents a spectrum of competing variations.

We have seen that historians differ greatly about how to practice historical scholarship and about the degree of objectivity that can plausibly be sought. Social-scientific interpretation should be mentioned here because it also deals with the text in light of its external context and, at least for some of its practitioners, wants to contribute to the historical understanding of the text. But it distinguishes itself from historical interpretation in that its conceptions are more systematic and explicitly theoretical than those of historians; and it seeks to articulate generalizations about social systems within which particular historical events and persons can be made understandable (Elliott 1986:5–6; Malina 1986:172–77).

The existential situation—or social location—from which interpretation can be made varies from a focus on the interior life of the individual to a focus on the individual and the social matrix in which the individual is inherently involved and by which he or she is stamped.

There are many types of literary criticism, which I very selectively and summarily mention. Formalistic literary criticism sees the text as autonomous, or semi-autonomous, in relation to author, reader, or historical context and focuses on the manifest surface form. Structuralist interpretation understands the surface of the text to be generated and governed by an abstract, deep structure that must be teased out of the surface specifics. Deconstruction erases the boundaries between putative texts, placing them all in one unbounded and encompassing super text, and sees the whole as a network of differential traces, having no origin and referring endlessly to each other. There is no structure or center, and language transgresses itself in that elements logically excluded from a discourse nevertheless reenter it. It should also be pointed out that literary critics will differ as to whether the emphasis falls on plot, metaphor, theme, character, irony, or other features.

I mention finally reader-response criticism, in the practice of which interpreters disagree on the magnitude of the reader's contribution to the meaning of the text. Reader-response criticism is the nodal point at which existential interpretation and literary criticism coalesce, for both of these give focal attention to the role of the reader-interpreter in creating meaning. What has happened in the last few decades is that the scope for describing the vantage point from which one reads has been greatly expanded, and within that enlarged discursive space numerous particular locations for reading have been articulated. Rudolf Bultmann defined the existential situation too much in individualistic terms, but Dorothee Soelle is right that Bultmann's strength was his principle that a theological statement should answer questions posed by the concrete situation. Political theology, therefore, draws the logical conclusion from Bultmann's situational thinking. Bultmann prompted the move from existential to political theology (Soelle 1974:2, 22). Now various political and liberationist theologies have emerged as particularizations of reader-response interpretation.

This last point could be put by saying that reader-response criticism has found amplification in cultural studies. Perhaps the main thrust of Stephen Moore's introduction to cultural studies in biblical studies is that cultural studies analyzes the role of the reader in his or her cultural/ideological context, focusing on how the culture—high or popular—influences the reception or appropriation of the Bible (Moore 1998:9, 11, 20–23). Cultural studies looks not only at the present culture of the interpreter but also at the past culture of the biblical text so that there is dynamic interaction between the two (Bach 1994:1).

An illuminating example of this is Ralph Broadbent's analysis of how several twentieth-century British historical critics treated some politically pertinent New Testament texts. These historical scholars were not as historical as they thought because *their* ideology kept them from seeing what was in the texts as embedded in the texts' own historical contexts. That is, their ideology derived from British public schools, classics, and Oxford and Cambridge inclined their exegesis to promote the concerns of the rich and powerful and to ignore or spiritualize those of the poor (Broadbent 1998:52–55). Thus identification of the bias of the interpreter gives us a better purchase on the historical import of the biblical text.

Kenneth Surin has argued that a Christian theological cultural criticism will employ the means of salvation to overcome the recalcitrant historical conditions that oppose liberation (2000:54).

Finally, I look selectively and summarily at several positions to read from that could be understood as particularizations of biblical cultural studies. Liberation theology broadly speaking interprets the Bible from the situation of the poor and marginalized—which includes both the self-understanding of the marginalized and the practice of opposing injustice as disciples to Jesus.

Feminist hermeneutics is the reading of a text (or writing an analysis or reconstructing a history) in light of the oppressive structures of a patriarchal society (Tolbert 1983:119). African American biblical hermeneutics reads from the vital life of the black church and against a racist society and Eurocentric hermeneutics (Felder 1991:6–7, 28).

Postcolonial criticism is not so much a method as a sensibility to a range of textual and historical phenomena generated by colonialism. As employed in New Testament interpretation it might ask, for instance, whether the Gospel of Mark offers a theological critique of Roman—and present-day—imperialism or rather substitutes an absolutist Jesus for an absolutist Rome (Moore 2000:183, 186–88). Or postcolonial interpretation might read from a complex location like present-day Hong Kong and reflect on the possible interaction between traditional Western critical scholarship and the newly arising consciousness emerging from postcolonial Asia (Lee 1999:156–60). R. S. Sugirtharajah's postcolonial Asian hermeneutics wants to use Asian cultural and social perspectives to illuminate biblical texts, recognizing the differences between the two but not subordinating one under the other (1994:251–58).

Gerald West and Musa W. Dube propose a reading process in which trained, critical biblical scholars read the Bible with poor, ordinary African readers. The subjectivities of both partners are taken seriously and foregrounded; the unequal power relations are acknowledged, as is the association of biblical criticism with global structures of dominance; the Bible is to be read from the perspective of the poor. Yet critical interpretation has a contribution to make to the situation of the poor—help in achieving a critical language or in making a critical language that they may already have more explicit and structured. Social transformation is the goal (West and Dube 1996:7, 12, 15; West 1996:26–32).

In sum, New Testament theological interpretation should engage in some way all four of the factors in the interpretive situation. But no scholar could or should be expected to actualize all—or necessarily many—of the variations. It is hoped, however, that the New Testament guild as a whole will keep all of the possibilities alive.

Works Cited

Adam, A. K. M. 1995a. *Making Sense of New Testament Theology: Modern Problems and Prospects.* Studies in American Biblical Hermeneutics 11. Macon, Ga.: Mercer Univ. Press.

———. 1995b. *What Is Postmodern Biblical Criticism?* Guides to Biblical Scholarship. Minneapolis: Fortress Press.

———, editor. 2000. *Handbook of Postmodern Biblical Interpretation.* St. Louis: Chalice.

Adorno, Theodor W. 1997. *The Jargon of Authenticity.* Translated by K. Tarnowski and F. Will. Evanston: Northwestern Univ. Press.

Altizer, Thomas J. J. 1990. "The Beginning and Ending of Revelation." In *Theology at the End of the Century: A Dialogue on the Postmodern.* Edited by R. P. Scharlemann, 76–109. Charlottesville: Univ. Press of Virginia.

Bach, Alice. 1994. "Skipping Across Borders." *Biblical Interpretation* 2:1–7.

Balla, Peter. 1997. *Challenges to New Testament Theology: An Attempt to Justify the Enterprise.* Peabody, Mass.: Hendrickson.

Barr, James. 1999. *The Concept of Biblical Theology: An Old Testament Perspective.* Minneapolis: Fortress Press.

Barzun, Jacques. 2000. *From Dawn to Decadence: 500 Years of Cultural Life. 1500 to the Present.* New York: HarperCollins.

Beckett, Samuel. 1954. *Waiting for Godot.* New York: Grove.

Berg, Temma. 1989. "Reading In/to Mark." *Semeia* 48:187–206.

Boers, Hendrikus. 1979. *What Is New Testament Theology?* Guides to Biblical Scholarship. Philadelphia: Fortress Press.

Braun, Herbert. 1965. "The Problem of a Theology of the New Testament." Translated by J. Sanders. *Journal for Theology and the Church* 1:169–83.

———. 1968. "The Meaning of the Christology of the New Testament." Translated by P. J. Achtemeier. *Journal for Theology and the Church* 5:89–127.

———. 1979. *Jesus of Nazareth.* Translated by E. Kalin. Philadelphia: Fortress Press.

Broadbent, Ralph. 1998. "Ideology, Culture, and British New Testament Studies: The Challenge of Cultural Studies." *Semeia* 82:33–61.

Brueggemann, Walter. 1997. *Theology of the Old Testament: Testimony, Dispute, Advocacy.* Minneapolis: Fortress Press.

Bultmann, Rudolf. 1951. *Theology of the New Testament,* vol. 1. Translated by K. Grobel. New York: Scribner.

———. 1954. "The New Testament and Mythology." In *Kerygma and Myth.* Edited by H.-W. Bartsch. Translated by R. H. Fuller, 1–44. London: SPCK.

———. 1955a. *Theology of the New Testament,* vol. 2. Translated by K. Grobel. London: SCM.

———. 1955b. "The Problem of Hermeneutics." In *Essays: Philosophical and Theological.* Translated by J. C. G. Greig, 234–61. New York: Macmillan.

———. 1958a. *Jesus and the Word.* Translated by L. Smith and E. Lanterno. New York: Scribner.

———. 1958b. *Jesus Christ and Mythology.* New York: Scribner.

———. 1960a. "A Chapter in the Problem of Demythologizing." In *New Testament Sidelights: Essays in Honor of Alexander Converse Purdy.* Edited by H. K. McArthur, 1–9. Hartford: Hartford Seminary Foundation Press.

———. 1960b. *Existence and Faith: Shorter Writings of Rudolf Bultmann.* Edited and translated by S. Odgen. New York: Meridian.

———. 1962a. "The Case for Demythologizing." In *Kerygma and Myth,* vol. 2. Edited by H.-W. Bartsch. Translated by R. H. Fuller, 181–94. London: SPCK.

———. 1962b. *History and Eschatology.* New York: Harper.

———. 1963. *The History of the Synoptic Tradition.* Translated by J. Marsh. New York: Harper and Row.

———. 1964. "The Primitive Christian Kerygma and the Historical Jesus." In *The Historical Jesus and the Kerygmatic Christ.* Edited and translated by C. Braaten and R. A. Harrisville Jr., 15–42. Nashville: Abingdon.

———. 1969. *Faith and Understanding*, vol. 1. Edited by R. W. Funk. Translated by L. P. Smith. New York: Harper & Row.

Caird, G. B. 1995. *New Testament Theology.* Completed and edited by L. D. Hurst. Oxford: Clarendon.

Calinescu, Matei. 1987. *Five Faces of Modernity: Modernism, Avant-garde, Decadence, Kitsch, Postmodernism.* Durham: Duke Univ. Press.

Caputo, John D. 1993. *Demythologizing Heidegger.* Indiana Series in the Philosophy of Religion. Bloomington: Indiana Univ. Press.

———. 1999. "Apostles of the Impossible." In *God, the Gift, and Postmodernism.* Edited by J. D. Caputo and M. Scanlon, 185–222. Indiana Series in the Philosophy of Religion. Bloomington: Indiana Univ. Press.

Caputo, John D., and Michael Scanlon. 1999. "Introduction." In *God, the Gift, and Postmodernism.* Edited by J. D. Caputo and M. Scanlon, 1–19. Indiana Series in the Philosophy of Religion. Bloomington: Indiana Univ. Press.

Childs, Brevard S. 1970. *Biblical Theology in Crisis.* Philadelphia: Westminster.

———. 1984. *The New Testament as Canon: An Introduction.* Philadelphia: Fortress Press.

Cousins, Mark. 1989. "The Practice of Historical Investigation." In *Post-Structuralism and the Question of History.* Edited by D. Attridge et al., 126–36. Cambridge: Cambridge Univ. Press.

Crossan, John Dominic. 1991. *The Historical Jesus: The Life of a Mediterranean Jewish Peasant.* San Francisco: HarperSanFrancisco.

———. 1994. *Jesus: A Revolutionary Biography.* San Francisco: HarperSanFrancisco.

———. 1999. "Our Own Faces in Deep Wells: A Future for Historical Jesus Research." In *God, the Gift, and Postmodernism.* Edited by J. D. Caputo and M. Scanlon, 282–310. Indiana Series in the Philosophy of Religion. Bloomington: Indiana Univ. Press.

Cullmann, Oscar. 1959. *The Christology of the New Testament.* Translated by S. Guthrie and C. Hall. New Testament Library. Philadelphia: Westminster.

———. 1967. *Salvation in History.* Translated by S. G. Sowers et al. New Testament Library. New York: Harper & Row.

Derrida, Jacques. 1970. "Structure, Sign, and Play in the Discourse of the Human Sciences." In *The Languages of Criticism and the Sciences of Man: The Structuralist Controversy.* Edited by R. Macksey and E. Donato, 247–65. Baltimore: Johns Hopkins Univ. Press.

———. 1979a. "Living On." In *Deconstruction and Criticism,* 75–176. New York: Seabury.

———. 1979b. *Speech and Phenomena.* Translated by D. Allison. Evanston: Northwestern Univ. Press.

———. 1980. *Of Grammatology.* Translated by G. C. Spivak. Baltimore: Johns Hopkins Univ. Press.

———. 1982. "On an Apocalyptic Tone Recently Adopted in Philosophy." *Semeia* 23:63–97.

———. 1998. "Faith and Knowledge: The Two Sources of 'Religion' at the Limits of Reason Alone." Translated by S. Weber. In *Religion.* Edited by J. Derrida and G. Vattimo, 1–78. Stanford: Stanford Univ. Press.

———. 1999. "Responses." In *God, the Gift, and Postmodernism.* Edited by J. D. Caputo and M. Scanlon, 42–46, 181–84. Indiana Series in the Philosophy of Religion. Bloomington: Indiana Univ. Press.

Dodd, C. H. 1936. *The Apostolic Preaching and Its Developments.* London: Hodder and Stoughton.

———. 1938. *History and the Gospel.* New York: Scribner.

———. 1953. *The Interpretation of the Fourth Gospel.* Cambridge: Cambridge Univ. Press.

———. 1961. *The Parables of the Kingdom.* Rev. ed. New York: Scribners.

Donahue, John R. 1989. "The Changing Shape of New Testament Theology." *Theological Studies* 50:314–35.

———. 1996. "The Literary Turn and New Testament Theology: Detour or New Direction?" *Journal of Religion* 76:250–75.

Dunn, James D. G. 1980. *Christology in the Making: A New Testa-*

ment Inquiry into the Origins of the Doctrine of the Incarnation.
Philadelphia: Westminster.

———. 1977. *Unity and Diversity in the New Testament.* Philadelphia: Westminster. Second ed. with new foreword, 1989.

Eagleton, Terry. 1997. *The Illusions of Postmodernism.* Oxford: Blackwell.

Elliott, John H. 1986. "Social-Scientific Criticism of the New Testament." *Semeia* 35:1–33.

Felder, Cain Hope, editor. 1991. *Stony the Road We Trod: African American Biblical Interpretation.* Minneapolis: Fortress Press.

Feuerbach, Ludwig. 1957. *The Essence of Christianity.* Translated by G. Eliot. New York: Harper and Brothers.

Fish, Stanley. 1980a. "Interpreting the Variorum." In *Reader-Response Criticism: From Formalism to Post-structuralism.* Edited by J. P. Tompkins, 164–84. Baltimore: Johns Hopkins Univ. Press.

———. 1980b. *Is There a Text in This Class? The Authority of Interpretive Communities.* Cambridge: Harvard Univ. Press.

Fowl, Stephen. 1995. "Texts Don't Have Ideologies." *Biblical Interpretation* 3:15–34.

Fuller, Reginald H. 1965. *The Foundations of New Testament Christology.* New York: Scribner.

———. 1989. "New Testament Theology." In *The New Testament and Its Modern Interpreters.* Edited by E. J. Epp and G. W. MacRae, 565–84. Philadelphia: Fortress Press.

Funk, Robert W. 1996. *Honest to Jesus: Jesus for a New Millennium.* San Francisco: HarperSanFrancisco.

Funk, Robert W., and Roy W. Hoover. 1993. *The Five Gospels: The Search for the Authentic Words of Jesus.* New Translation and Commentary. New York: Macmillan.

Gabler, J. P. 1980. "On the Proper Distinction between Biblical and Dogmatic Theology and the Specific Objectives of Each." In John Sandys-Wunsch and Laurence Eldredge, translators, "J. P. Gabler and the Distinction between Biblical and Dogmatic

Theology: Translation, Commentary, and Discussion of His Originality." *Scottish Journal of Theology* 33:133–58.

Hahn, Ferdinand. 1969. *The Titles of Jesus in Christology: Their History in Early Christianity.* Translated by H. Knight and G. Ogg. New York: World. German ed. 1963.

Harvey, Barry. 2000. "Anti-postmodernism." In *Handbook of Postmodern Biblical Interpretation.* Edited by A. K. M. Adam, 1–7. St. Louis: Chalice.

Hasel, Gerhard F. 1978. *New Testament Theology: Basic Issues in the Current Debate.* Grand Rapids: Eerdmans.

Hassan, Ihab. 1987. *The Postmodern Turn: Essays in Postmodern Theory and Culture.* Columbus: Ohio State Univ. Press.

Hauerwas, Stanley. 1993. *Unleashing the Scripture: Freeing the Bible from Captivity to America.* Nashville: Abingdon.

———. 1999. "Surviving Postmodernism: The University, the Global Market, and Christian Narrative." *Soundings* 82:107–25.

Heidegger, Martin. 1962. *Being and Time.* Translated by J. Macquarrie and E. Robinson. New York: Harper & Row.

Ingraffia, Brian D. 1995. *Postmodern Theory and Biblical Theology: Vanquishing God's Shadow.* Cambridge: Cambridge Univ. Press.

Iser, Wolfgang. 1980. *The Act of Reading: A Theory of Aesthetic Response.* Baltimore: Johns Hopkins Univ. Press.

Jacobson, Roman. 1972. "Linguistics and Poetics." In *The Structuralists from Marx to Lévi-Strauss.* Edited by R. T. De George and F. M. De George, 85–112. Garden City, N.Y.: Doubleday.

Jameson, Fredric. 1984a. "Foreword." In Jean-François Lyotard, *The Postmodern Condition.* Translated by G. Bennington and B. Massum, vii–xxi. Minneapolis: Univ. of Minnesota Press.

———. 1984b. "Postmodernism, or the Cultural Logic of Late Capitalism." *New Left Review* 146:53–92.

———. 1989. "Afterword—Marxism and Postmodernism." In *Postmodernism.* Edited by D. Kellner, 369–87. Washington D.C.: Maisonneuve.

Jeremias, Joachim. 1963. *The Parables of Jesus.* Translated by S. H. Hooke. New York: Scribner. Rev. ed. 1972.

———. 1964. *The Problem of the Historical Jesus.* Translated by N. Perrin. Facet Books, Biblical Series 13. Philadelphia: Fortress. Reprinted as "The Search for the Historical Jesus," in *Jesus and the Message of the New Testament.* Edited by K. C. Hanson, 1–17. Fortress Classics in Biblical Studies. Minneapolis: Fortress Press, 2002.

———. 1965. *The Central Message of the New Testament.* New York: Scribner. Reprinted as "The Central Message of the New Testament," in *Jesus and the Message of the New Testament.* Edited by K. C. Hanson, 63–110. Fortress Classics in Biblical Studies. Minneapolis: Fortress Press, 2002.

———. 1971. *New Testament Theology.* Translated by J. Bowden. New York: Scribner.

Jones, Gareth. 1991. *Bultmann: Towards a Critical Theology.* Cambridge, Eng.: Polity.

Jonge, Marinus de. 1988. *Christology in Context.* Philadelphia: Westminster.

Käsemann, Ernst. 1969a. "The Beginnings of Christian Theology." In *New Testament Questions of Today.* Translated by W. J. Montague, 82–107. Philadelphia: Fortress Press.

———. 1969b. "Blind Alleys in the 'Jesus of History' Controversy." In *New Testament Questions of Today.* Translated by W. J. Montague, 23–65. Philadelphia: Fortress Press.

———. 1969c. "On the Subject of Primitive Christian Apocalyptic." In *New Testament Questions of Today.* Translated by W. J. Montague, 108–37. Philadelphia: Fortress Press.

———. 1973. "The Problem of a New Testament Theology." *New Testament Studies* 19:235–45.

Keck, Leander E. 1986. "Toward the Renewal of New Testament Christology." *New Testament Studies* 32:362–77.

Kellner, Hans. 1989. *Language and Historical Representation: Getting the Story Crooked.* Rhetoric of the Human Sciences. Madison: Univ. of Wisconsin Press.

Kermode, Frank. 1971. *Modern Essays*. London: Fontana.

———. 1979. *The Genesis of Secrecy: On the Interpretation of Narrative*. Cambridge: Harvard Univ. Press.

Koester, Helmut. 1983. *Introduction to the New Testament*. Vol. 2: *History and Literature of Early Christianity*. Philadelphia: Fortress Press.

Kort, Wesley A. 1996. *Take, Read: Scripture, Textuality, and Cultural Practice*. University Park: Pennsylvania State Univ. Press.

Leavey, John P. 1982. "Four Protocols: Derrida, His Deconstruction." *Semeia* 23:42–57.

Lee, Archie C. C. 1999. "Returning to China: Biblical Interpretation in Postcolonial Hong Kong." *Biblical Interpretation* 7:156–73.

Lyotard, Jean-François. 1984. *The Postmodern Condition: A Report on Knowledge*. Translated by G. Bennington and B. Massum. Minneapolis: Univ. of Minnesota Press.

Mack, Burton L. 1973. *Logos und Sophia: Untersuchungen zur Weisheitstheologie im hellenistischen Judentum*. Studien zur Umwelt des Neuen Testaments 10. Göttingen: Vandenhoeck & Ruprecht.

———. 1988. *A Myth of Innocence: Mark and Christian Origins*. Philadelphia: Fortress Press.

Malina, Bruce J. 1986. "The Received View and What It Cannot Do." *Semeia* 35:171–94. Reprinted in *The Social World of Jesus and the Gospels*, 217–41. London: Routledge, 1996.

Marxsen, Willi. 1979. *The Beginnings of Christology*. Translated by P. J. Achtemeier and L. Nieting. Philadelphia: Fortress Press.

Matera, Frank J. 1999. *New Testament Christology*. Louisville: Westminster John Knox.

McKnight, Edgar V. 1994. "A Sheep in Wolf's Clothing: An Option in Contemporary New Testament Hermeneutics." In *The New Literary Criticism and the New Testament*. Edited by E. S. Malbon and E. V. McKnight, 326–47. JSNT Supplement Series 109. Sheffield: Sheffield Academic.

Montrose, Louis. 1989. "Professing the Renaissance: The Poetics and Politics of Culture." In *The New Historicism*. Edited by H. A. Veeser, 15–36. London: Routledge.

Moore, Stephen D. 1998. "Between Birmingham and Jerusalem: Cultural Studies and Biblical Studies." *Semeia* 82:1–32.

———. 2000. "Postcolonialism." In *Handbook of Postmodern Biblical Interpretation*. Edited by A. K. M. Adam, 182–88. St. Louis: Chalice.

Morgan, Robert. 1973. *The Nature of New Testament Theology*. Studies in Biblical Theology 2/25. London: SCM.

Perrin, Norman. 1976. *Jesus and the Language of the Kingdom: Symbol and Metaphor in New Testament Interpretation*. Philadelphia: Fortress Press.

———. 1984. "Jesus and the Theology of the New Testament." *Journal of Religion* 64:413–31.

Plato. *Timaeus*.

Räisänen, Heikki. 1990. *Beyond New Testament Theology: A Story and a Programme*. Philadelphia: Trinity.

———. 2000. "Biblical Criticism in the Global Village." In *Reading the Bible in the Global Village*, 9–28. Atlanta: Society of Biblical Literature.

Reiss, Timothy J. 1982. *The Discourse of Modernism*. Ithaca, N.Y.: Cornell Univ. Press.

Ricoeur, Paul. 1976. *Interpretation Theory: Discourse and the Surplus of Meaning*. Fort Worth: Texas Christian Univ. Press.

Robbe-Grillet, Alain. 1965. *For a New Novel: Essays on Fiction*. Translated by R. Howard. New York: Grove.

Robinson, James M. 1976. "The Future of New Testament Theology." *Religious Studies Review* 2:17–23.

Rorty, Richard. 1997. "Lofty Ideas That May Be Losing Altitude." *The New York Times* B, 13:3, November 1.

Saussure, Ferdinand de. 1966. *Course in General Linguistics*. Translated by W. Baskin. New York: McGraw-Hill.

Scharlemann, Robert P., editor. 1990. *Theology at the End of the*

Century: A Dialog on the Postmodern. Studies in Religion and Culture. Charlottesville: Univ. Press of Virginia.

Schmithals, Walter. 1997. *The Theology of the First Christians.* Translated by O. C. Dean Jr. Louisville: Westminster John Knox. German ed. 1994.

Scholes, Robert. 1985. *Textual Power: Literary Theory and the Teaching of English.* New Haven: Yale Univ. Press.

Scroggs, Robin. 1988. "Can New Testament Theology Be Saved? The Threat of Contextualisms." *Union Seminary Quarterly Review* 42:17–31.

Sherwood, Yvonne. 2000. "Derrida." In *Handbook of Postmodern Interpretation.* Edited by A. K. M. Adam, 69–75. St. Louis: Chalice.

Soelle, Dorothee. 1974. *Political Theology.* Translated by J. Shelley. Philadelphia: Fortress Press.

Stendahl, Krister. 1962. "Biblical Theology, Contemporary." In *The Interpreter's Dictionary of the Bible.* Edited by G. A. Buttrick, 1.418–32. Nashville: Abingdon.

———. 1965. "Method in the Study of Biblical Theology." In *The Bible in Modern Scholarship.* Edited by J. P. Hyatt, 196–216. Nashville: Abingdon.

———. 2000. "Dethroning Biblical Imperialism in Theology." In *Reading the Bible in the Global Village,* 61–66. Atlanta: Society of Biblical Literature.

Stout, Jeffrey. 1982. "What Is the Meaning of a Text?" *New Literary History* 14:1–12.

Strecker, Georg. 2000. *Theology of the New Testament.* Translated by M. E. Boring. Louisville: Westminster John Knox. German ed. 1996.

Sugirtharajah, R. S. 1994. "Introduction, and Some Thoughts on Asian Biblical Hermeneutics." *Biblical Interpretation* 23:251–63.

Surin, Kenneth. 2000. "Culture/Cultural Criticism." In *Handbook of Postmodern Biblical Interpretation.* Edited by A. K. M. Adam, 49–54. St. Louis: Chalice.

Taylor, Mark C. 1990a. "Nothing Ending Nothing." In *Theology at the End of the Century: A Dialogue on the Postmodern.* Edited by R. P. Scharlemann, 41–75. Charlottesville: Univ. Press of Virginia.

———. 1990b. "Unending Strokes." In *Theology at the End of the Century: A Dialogue on the Postmodern*. Edited by R. P. Scharlemann, 136–48. Charlottesville: Univ. Press of Virginia.

Tolbert, Mary Ann. 1983. "Defining the Problem: The Bible and Feminist Hermeneutics." *Semeia* 28:113–26.

Via, Dan O. 1985. *The Ethics of Mark's Gospel—In the Middle of Time*. Philadelphia: Fortress Press.

———. 1990. *Self-Deception and Wholeness in Paul and Matthew*. Minneapolis: Fortress Press.

———. 1997. *The Revelation of God and/as Human Reception*. Harrisburg, Pa.: Trinity Press International.

West, Gerald. 1996. "Reading the Bible Differently: Giving Shape to the Discourses of the Dominated." *Semeia* 73:21–41.

West, Gerald, and Musa W. Dube. 1996. "An Introduction: How We Have Come to 'Read With.'" *Semeia* 73:7–17.

White, Hayden. 1978. *Tropics of Discourse: Essays in Cultural Criticism*. Baltimore: Johns Hopkins Univ. Press.

———. 1989a. "'Figuring the nature of the times deceased': Literary Theory and Historical Writing." In *The Future of Literary Theory*. Edited by R. Cohen, 19–43. London: Routledge.

———. 1989b. "The New Historicism: A Comment." In *The New Historicism*. Edited by H. A. Veeser, 293–302. London: Routledge.

———. 1990. *The Content of the Form: Narrative Discourse and Historical Representation*. Baltimore: Johns Hopkins Univ. Press.

Wrede, William. 1973. "The Task and Methods of 'New Testament Theology.'" In *The Nature of New Testament Theology*. Edited by R. Morgan, 68–116. Studies in Biblical Theology 2/25. London: SCM.

Wright, N. T. 1992. *The New Testament and the People of God*. Minneapolis: Fortress Press.

———. 1996. *Jesus and the Victory of God*. Minneapolis: Fortress Press.

———. 1999a. "Born of a Virgin?" In Marcus J. Borg and N. T. Wright, *The Meaning of Jesus: Two Visions*, 171–78. San Francisco: HarperSanFrancisco.

———. 1999b. "The Transforming Reality of the Bodily Resurrection." In Marcus J. Borg and N. T. Wright, *The Meaning of Jesus: Two Visions*, 111–27. San Francisco: HarperSanFrancisco.

Author Index

Scripture Index